# REVOLUTION
## ON CANVAS

### VOLUME 2

D0951626

# REVOLUTION
## ON CANVAS

**VOLUME 2**

### POETRY FROM
### THE INDIE MUSIC SCENE

EDITED BY
## RICH BALLING

**WARNER BOOKS**

NEW YORK    BOSTON

Warner Books
Hachette Book Group USA
237 Park Avenue
New York, NY 10169

Visit our Web site at www.HachetteBookGroupUSA.com.

Printed in the United States of America

First Edition: May 2007

10 9 8 7 6 5 4 3 2 1

ISBN: 978-0-446-69787-3
LCCN: 2005937223

To my father and mother,

Richard and Linda Balling

# TABLE OF CONTENTS

Foreword   xv

**JUSTIN PIERRE**
Motion City Soundtrack

*Annalisa*   1

**JONAH MATRANGA**

*Speech to Text, Thought
   to Action*   9

**REBEKAH JORDAN**
Dreaming Ferns

*"I am right-handed."*   11

**JOHN TRAN**
Home Grown/Red Panda

*About Me:*   14

**BRENDAN BROWN**
The Receiving End of Sirens

*"Of ritual and habit I opened
   my mouth"*   15

**SCHUYLAR CROOM**
He Is Legend

*Letter to a Gypsy*   16

**VINCENT REYES**
Create!

*Lao-tzu and a Friend Play
   a Game of Marbles*   18
*Dalí*   20

**MEG FRAMPTON**
Meg & Dia

*"For the first time, this
   sickness . . ."*   21

DIA FRAMPTON
Meg & Dia

Hospitals Always Smell Like
    Decaying Hair   23

JOSH PARTINGTON
Firescape/Something
  Corporate

27 Hours   26
Orchids   27

JARED DRAUGHON
Classic Case

New York City Vampires   28
Human Error   29

COLLEEN NAPOLITANO

The Study   30

RICH BALLING
The Sound of Animals
  Fighting

Einstein on the Beach   32
Werner Herzog   33
Sarah Kane   34
H. P. Lovecraft   35
Calvino   36
Celine   37

JASON GLEASON
ActionReaction

For the Day   38
It May as Well Have Been
    March 21, 1982.   39
If Humans Have Heartbeats,
    Do Robots Have Heartbeeps?   41

ALEXANDER KENT
Say Anything

A Short Clip from "The Unlike-
    liness of Counterpane"   43

JARROD TAYLOR
In Reverent Fear

A Young Mother's Medicine   48

BEN JORGENSEN
Armor For Sleep

The Big Reveal   50

RICH PALMER
Buddhah

Do What You Need to Be Happy   51

PORTER MCKNIGHT
Atreyu

"Come tell me old man"   53

KIRK HUFFMAN
Gatsbys American Dream

"My apartment was muggy
    when I awoke"   55

**ALEX HOVIS**
Paper Models

*Never Forget Her*   57

**GRETA SALPETER**
The Hush Sound

*You are the moon*   58
*New Year's Eve*   59

**ROB MORRIS**
The Hush Sound

*the mess i've made for you*   60
*the sinking of some great ship*   63

**SCOTT WALDMAN**
The City Drive

*Is Bette Midler a True Star?*   65

**DANNY SMITH**
The City Drive

*Hesperia*   66

**TRAVIS BRYANT**
Goodbye Tomorrow

*save the boy*   68
*missouri*   69

**AARON CHAPMAN**
Nurses

*"I spoke with GOD last
   night . . ."*   71

**DAMON DAW**
Nurses

*Musicalism*   73

**KENNY VASOLI**
The Starting Line

*My Flaws Get Along*   76

**ELGIN JAMES**
Dream Weaver

*"I was eight years old
   when . . ."*   77

**AARON BEDARD**
Bane

*One Summer Knight*   85

**RYAN HUNTER**
Envy on the Coast

*Auditions with Our Heavenly
   Father*   102

**SAL BOSSIO**
Envy on the Coast

*My heart is pounding the whole
   way there.*   104

**PETER WENTZ**
Fall Out Boy

*"Tonight we lie in a city . . ."*   105

**CHINA SOUL**
Minor Celebration

*Dramatic Monologue*   109

**MATTHEW ROSKOWSKI**
Delilah in the Calm

*Roll Up My Sympathy* 111

**MATTHEW CLEGG**
Caitlin Going and the
  All the Way's

*Which Way?* 112

**MARK ROSE**
Spitalfield

*Vocals/Guitar* 113

**STEVE LEFEBVRE**
Sophia

*feeding bob potter* 114

**CHI CHENG**
Deftones

*The Death of a Family Guilt* 115
*Murder, Prostitution and Other
  Forms of Democracy and the
  Institution of Marriage* 118

**BRANDON WRONSKI**
Dead Letter Diaries

*Progress in Part* 120
*Sand in Context* 121
*Kodiak* 122

**ADAM PANIC**
Adam Panic

*Hello me.* 124

**JOHN NOLAN**
Straylight Run

*I Might Be Wrong* 125

**SHAWN HARRIS**
The Matches

*My Doe* 132

**RYAN TRASTER**
Small Towns Burn
  a Little Slower

*Death Rattle* 135

**JON TUMMILLO**
Folly

*This Is Exactly What It Doesn't Feel
  Like to Be in Space* 136

**GABE SAPPORTA**
Cobra Starship

*Success* 138
*It's Warmer in the Basement* 139

**JOE BROWN**
A Static Lullaby

*Lola and Gus* 141

STEVE CHOI
Rx Bandits
*Purge*   142
*Blah*   143

MATT EMBREE
Rx Bandits
*"Well it's coming down to it"*   144

BOBBY DARLING
Gatsbys American Dream
*The Museum*   147

M. S. BREEN
Emanuel
*"with your legs spread . . ."*   148
*my anapex.*   150

AARON BARRETT
Reel Big Fish
*Tastes Like Christmas*   151

ADAM TURLA
Murder by Death
*Spring #1*   152

CHRIS FRANGICETTO
Days Away
*"we live in shadow, we grow immune"*   153

STEVE ELKINS
The Autumns
*One Central Fire Against Two Craters: Part One*   157

DANIEL BARRON
Dollar Fifty Date
*Purgatory at the Jersey Shore*   164

JERRY JONES
Trophy Scars
*Jerry and Jerry Go for a Drive*   167

BRANDON RIKE
Dead Poetic
*We Are Vultures*   170

NICK MARTIN
Underminded
*I'm committed to safe driving*   171
*Drugs VS. The Patriot VS. Paris*   172

EVAN JEWETT
Worker Bee
*loss of a squirt gun—*   174
*lost keys—*   175

DUANE OKEN
Socratic
*Honorable Discharge*   177

**NICK THOMAS**
The Spill Canvas

*Galaxy Eater*   178

**ERIC VICTORINO**
Strata

*Stray Bullet Effect*   179

**BRIAN TASCH**
Boy Armageddon

*"tonight"*   181

**BOB NANNA**
The City on Film

*"This is what I do . . ."*   182

**CRAIG OWENS**
Chiodos

*"when i sleep . . ."*   187

**JESSE KURVINK**
HelloGoodbye

*I love you and I miss you*
*    all the time*   188

**KELCEY AYER**
Cavil at Rest

*The Heat Lamp*   189

**DAN LYMAN**
Halos

*"Loud bang at the window."*   191

**KERRY TRUSEWICZ**
Royden

*Sometimes I Travel to You*   192

**CHRISTOPHER JAMES RUFF**
Kaddisfly

*Waves*   194
*The Calm of Calamity*   196
*Osmosis*   197
*Alone as a Tree?*   198

**DANIEL MURILLO**
Lorene Drive

*For the Rest of Us*   201

**COLIN FRANGICETTO**
Circa Survive

*"HUMILIATING SOBRIETY" and*
*    the MISSING LIMB*
*    (a godless prayer)*   202

**ANTHONY GREEN**
Circa Survive

*Look—Look*   207

**BRENDAN EKSTROM**
Circa Survive

*". . ."*   208

**ERIC FREDERIC**
Facing New York

*"hands are lightbulbs"*   209

**MATTHEW KELLY**
The Autumns

*The Pale Antechamber*   211

**DAVID MELILLO**

*"I went down to the bar . . ."*   217
*"It always burns . . ."*   218
*"This apathy . . ."*   219

**TIM MCILRATH**
Rise Against

*babygirl*   220

**MIKE MADRUGA**
Fear Before the March
   of Flames

*Owl Farm*   222

**LUIS DUBUC**
The Secret Handshake

*Last Day Alive*   224

# FOREWORD

In the seventh grade, I was the next Melville. My sophomore year in high school, everything changed.

Papers I pained over came back littered with holierthanthou jargon that was nearly indecipherable. What comments I could read, I wished I could not. The verdict was in: the pen truly was mightier than the sword. The same vehicle that brought forth the thoughtful writing of students was being misused to etch careless comment-graffiti onto their papers, causing many like myself to close up and not explore true potential. I was sure that nowhere in the English-teacher handbook was there a clause that instructed ridding the world of potentially brilliant authors by way of red ink. In fact, I could attest that a little positive recognition went ten times further than reckless criticism. What had I written that had been so bad? One year earlier, I'm certain I would have won the "Most Likely to Write the Next *Leaves of Grass*" award. I spent the remainder of my high school career afraid to make a wrong move, weary of thinking outside the box. College was a clean slate and stirred some realizations.

Growing up, there were always books around. Lining hall-way shelves was everything from *Goodnight Moon* to the Holy Bible. In hindsight, I feel the density of the latter had a great something to do with me making significant headway in my early literacy development. Headway that would eventually be impaled by the William Somerset Maughams of my high school curriculum and the aforementioned red ink. The only clear and pleasant memory of high school was Mr. Brown, who would dress as Edgar Allan Poe for Halloween and read "The Raven" in character.

My passion for writing was first unearthed in college. After a brief stint in a mortuary science program, I thought creative writing sounded like fun. John Payne, who wrote the introduction to volume one of this series, was my professor for two semesters of creative writing and allowed me plenty of room to experiment and find my voice. He had graduated from Cal State Long Beach, and played a critical role in my decision to transfer there. He was also the one to recommend *The Girl in the Flammable Skirt* by Aimee Bender, which, to this day is a favorite book, and one that continues to aid my own writing.

Though the stories of Bender, Bukowski, Camus, and others have impacted my own writing, nothing has cultivated my literacy more than music. The same solace found in books by most life-long readers, I find in the liner notes of CDs. As a soon-to-be teen in junior high, lyrics taught me vocabulary, poetic form, how to rhyme, wordplay, and much more. The music of Bob Dylan, Marvin Gaye, the Rolling Stones, etc., told me stories and used melody to drive those stories into my head. And there they would stay, encouraging my individual growth and inviting imitation.

I followed the dream of becoming a professional musician

after high school when the trombone I had played since the fourth grade enabled me to tour in a band. Every other semester throughout my years at Cypress College, I went on tour, traveling nine times through every single state and once through Europe, playing to countless kids each night. I saw firsthand how many people other than myself found music to be spiritual and that it wasn't just me finding so much passion in melodies and the words that complement them.

Enter 2003. The idea was to contact numerous musicians that I had shared floors and crossed borders with during my years of touring—many of whom had since grown to be extremely popular and had sold hundreds of thousands of records—and gather writing from them. Lyrics that had never made it into songs, journal entries, poems, fiction, essays, rants, and even art were collected from nearly eighty musicians. The vision was to make reading approachable to a large number of people who never got excited by the likes of Wordsworth and Coleridge in school and to those that were disgusted by the heightened focus of image over quality content in music. I wanted to show that poetry was, and always will be, capable of engaging even the most apathetic of minds, and that people we all listened to on our stereos wrote poetry. The book, *Revolution on Canvas*, was released on Valentine's Day 2004, and in your hands is the all-new second volume. The Ad Astra Books team still receives letters from those that have bought the first book, one of which had written on the envelope, "I just realized this is the first time I'm writing a letter to share the fact I love a book." A single letter like that validates every second of hard work spent.

Thank you for furthering your own journey to lifelong literacy along with me, through your support of this book. The fact that you are reading this right now is evidence of a hunger for moving the spotlight back onto the words that change lives and shape songs and away from the image-centered mind-set placed on world art by a blind industry.

Blessings,
Rich Balling

# REVOLUTION
## ON CANVAS

### VOLUME 2

**JUSTIN PIERRE**
`Motion City Soundtrack`

## *Annalisa*

The first time I met her I was in the middle of a three-day binge. I had worked my way out of bed around noon and walked the ten and a half blocks down Franklin to Mortimer's. Mort's was where I spent most of my drinking time, as nobody I knew would be caught dead there. Thus there was no chance of running into someone who would squeal to the band about my extracurricular activities. For this particular drunk I chose scotch. I was in a Bukowski phase at the time. I spent most of the day writing lyrics and ordered a Boca burger around five. I was sitting on the lower level of the bar. There is an elevated portion they open up after six for the post-work rush. She came in through the side door. She was wearing a blue sequined tube dress. It was obnoxious and it cast a laser light show all around the dim dining area. She ordered a few drinks and carried them over to a table near me. She had quite a mane of dirty blond hair that jostled about as she sank into her seat. I remember asking her, "Why all the beer?"

"Happy hour." She did have two of every kind, six bottles in all. She smiled at me and winked. Her makeup was a mess—all blues and blacks smeared every which way. She lit a cigarette—menthol, of course. I tried my hand at conversation. "I've been coming here for months and they never told me about any goddamn happy hour."

"That's because they're selfish and want it all to themselves." She had already finished two of the six bottles on her table.

"Sounds like a bad business move if you ask me." She reminded me of that actress Jane Adams, only with dirty blond hair. She was very skinny and sexy in a skeletal sort of way. We talked for another hour or so as she drank her beer and I downed my two-for-one scotch and waters. I normally don't smoke, but when I get drunk I tend to break all the rules. She was very generous with her Newport Lights. When the upstairs opened up, we went there and hid out in the corner at a table with minimal light. Turns out she was thirty-six, ten years older than me at the time, and cut hair at Great Clips. She modeled on the side for extra cash, which I assumed explained her outfit. We talked about her various boyfriends, her two cats Camilla and Neptune, and how hard it was to break into the acting business in Minneapolis. She had done a local spot for Jake's Bar a few years ago which she wasn't too proud of but she made two thousand dollars in residuals from it.

After a few more hours of drunken conversation, she suggested that we go back to her place. I had nothing better to do so I agreed to accompany her. We walked out of Mortimer's and into the Wedge parking lot. She was searching violently through her purse. She stopped at a teal Neon that was in pretty good shape on the outside, but the inside was total carnage.

"Fucking keys!" I always thought it was funny when people yelled at inanimate objects. I wandered around to the passenger side and looked through the window. There were several empty bottles of vodka on the passenger-side floor. The back was full of pillows and clothes covered in cat hair. Cigarette butts spilled out over the ashtray and into the parking brake area. I noticed the keys were still dangling in the ignition. I opened the door, which was unlocked, and grabbed the keys. She was sitting on the pavement sifting through all her belongings, having dumped them out of the purse. I handed her the keys. She gave me a questioning look, then threw all of her junk back into the purse and hopped in the car. Even though it's pretty fucked up, I have to say that one of my favorite things to do is drive drunk. I'm a nervous person by trade and after I've had a few, I find that my nerves seem to be calmed enough to deal with the human race. However, being a passenger in a car driven by a drunk woman in her mid-thirties with several boyfriends and two cats is not a good way to calm your nerves, even after ingesting half a bottle of J&B. We made it to her house eventually. Even though it was only ten blocks away, it took us thirty-five minutes as she got lost several times and was confused as to whether it was okay to drive through red lights after stopping if nobody else is around.

She introduced me to her cats as though they were people. They were fat. I didn't care for them and they sure as hell didn't care for me. She opened up a bottle of cheap red wine, the kind with the kangaroo on it. Her place was a dump. It was like her car, only bigger and shittier. Her CD player was a boombox. She had no DVD player. Everything had dust on it and the whole place smelled of cat piss. I kind of felt bad for her in a way. Here I was, slumming it. I had a nice apartment, a kick-ass job and lots of toys. She had a VCR and a few uninteresting stories she told over and over and over . . .

We did end up fooling around. But the thing about drunk people is that we're never really committed to the moment one hundred percent. It's like watching two coma patients come out of it and fumble around for floppy penis and bone-dry vagina. After a half hour of bliss we went back to the bottle. Our relationship was solidified. I was her personal confidant and she was the drunk of my dreams, the only girl who could suck it down faster than I could.

It occurred to me the morning after that first night I had forgotten to ask what her name was. Typical. We cleared it up as I ran into her several times over the next few months. Her name was Annalisa. She pronounced Anna like the word *father*, with an *ahh* sound. So debonair. We spent most of our time together at Mortimer's or the small bar attached to its side called Gringo's. Gringo's was a faux-Mexican joint, modern crappy artwork and paintwork resembling things you'd see at roadside truck stops in Arizona. For some reason all the hipsters filtered into there on the weekends when they couldn't get into the Red Dragon across the street. Perhaps it was the ambiance. The owner was the only white man with an Afro I'd ever seen other than the Greatest American Hero. His name was Dave. I called him Super Dave, on account of he was that awesome. He was always in a good mood and always remembered my usual like I was a real barfly. I loved him for that. He and Annalisa went way back and they were close in age. It was wonderful to hear stories about the Replacements and Soul Asylum and Minneapolis in the late '80s before I was old enough to know any better about music. Unfortunately Super Dave's taste in music had plummeted in the last decade, as all the music played at Gringo's was crap—bad metal bands doing their best Pantera impersonations and failing miserably. Those blessed drunken nights always ended the same. Annalisa and I would end up at her place after last call and we'd drink until she passed out and I would walk home as the sun woke the whole state.

Eventually I had to go back out on tour. The band I was in had recently gotten signed and our time off had come to an end as our first record was about to be released. I curbed the drinking habit pretty well while on the road, with only a few minor fuckups. I did see significantly less of Annalisa over the next few years. I'd get random drunken phone calls from her on the road beckoning me to come down to Mort's or Gringo's to have a nightcap, and by nightcap she meant "sauce-a-thon." It would just about break my heart. As soon as I would return from a tour, I was down at Mort's first thing and eventually she would show and we would pick up right where we left off. For the most part, nothing changed. There was only one time we decided to do something other than go to the bar. We went to the midnight movie at the Uptown Theatre one Saturday night. *Blue Velvet* was showing and we were both David Lynch fans so we drank up before and drove down there. We got kicked out ten minutes into the film when Annalisa accidentally lit up a cigarette and they discovered the better half of a twelve-pack we had smuggled in by way of our jacket pockets. That was the first and last time we ventured further than a ten-block radius from Mort's.

Tours came and went, as did my time with Annalisa. We saw less and less of each other as the months turned into a year and so forth. One time I came back to Minneapolis and couldn't get ahold of her. I spent nearly a week at the bar but she never showed. I asked Super Dave about her, but he didn't have any information. Eventually, she showed up one night. She looked like hell. It was as if she had aged several years in the last few months since I had seen her. She lit up when she saw me and we drank and conversed for a bit. But it wasn't the same. She wasn't there. When it came to about midnight she said she had to leave. This had never happened before. I was kind of put off by this sudden change in behavior but there wasn't much I could do about it. She kissed me on the cheek and bounced out of there. I drank and I drank until I had to pee, then I drank some more and somehow made my way to her place and passed out on the doorstep. Near morning she woke me and invited me in. We drank wine and ate bagels.

"Here's the story," she began, "Hank is my sugar daddy, for lack of a better way of explaining things. He pays the rent and I just have to show up and spend time with him every now and again." And then I was all sorts of pissed off.

"The way you say it, it's like you think I think you're cheating on me. I'm not a fucking child. I just miss my drinking buddy."

"Hey," she yelled, "I'm not the one who's never around. You show up when it's convenient for you." She had a point there. "You're not that goddamned original. I've known dozens of people just like you who come and go at their convenience."

"There's no need to get nasty." I truly didn't know what to say. We just sat there for a while waiting for the world to wake up.

"Look, I gotta go to work in a few hours." I got the hint, put on my jacket and left with my bagel. That was the last time I saw her.

She uncovered the lid on me. It's true. I used people much like I used the drink. I didn't think there was anything wrong with what I was doing since we weren't fucking each other, but emotionally I was just one in a long line of rapists. It upsets me that she had me figured out on day one but said nothing. It makes me think I've greatly underestimated the human race. I tried calling for several months, but she never answered. I left messages while on tour but never got a response. One day, almost a year after our final incident, I walked into Gringo's. I hadn't had much time off as it had been a good year. Super Dave was still there and bad music still played. He brought me my scotch and water with a little wave of the hand like a magician, for effect. I hadn't seen him in a while. I sat and I drank and I waited. I drank and I drank and I drank. It was nearing eleven or twelve something and I asked Super Dave about her, if she still came around or what the shit the deal was with her.

"Oh, she's dead," he said, "yeah, like two months ago they found her in her apartment. She'd hung herself."

He went on to help someone else. I could feel my hair growing. That's strange, I thought. I drank until I could no longer hear myself think. The next morning I was shaking. Strange, I thought. I drank a few shots to calm down, and eventually the bottle was gone.

Whether you know from personal experience or not, whether in bar rooms or meetings across America where people chain-smoke and devour coffee—the stories are always the same. If and when you become a part of the drinking life, you step into a world where people you hardly know become your best friends and your best friends become people you hardly know. I didn't know her, but I knew her and to this day I still miss her. It's funny, the deeper you swim, the harder it is to surface. Eventually you just want to stay down there at the bottom and drown. As diverse as we in the drinking life are, there is truly only one thing we all have in common: a lot of dead friends.

—justin pierre.

## JONAH MATRANGA

### *Speech to Text, Thought to Action*

Disease is vote reinsurer
hundred sure her hair ornament a gonna a a a a a a a
on auto are high
I'm Donna and Pat at of the average of

of what
of the shorter the learned
of the
of the date
of revenue creative
of the current climate
of and as the deal will result
of those voting machines so
of the causes
of the vote
of this everyone within this set of
of what with was so excessive in the above of

and I was a kid going back and forth.
The those in Idaho, and of the drugs of the vote
and partisan now
Steven of is extremely close it down
and tell the bereaved of its heavy overseas valve in the matter

how close is as one died or been given until next president of
United States with her family
and if he's the these there is evident from the House official
how I think he's love
of is that what with his resolve the be debated forever
whose shadow of legitimacy of this House and all we have to
help him

## REBEKAH JORDAN
Dreaming Ferns

I am right-handed. I wish I were ambidextrous. I can only wink my right eye. I prefer Twizzlers to Red Vines. Fall is my favorite season. I had a love affair with the leaves. I liked to collect them, trace them on paper. I liked to step on them and hear them crackle. I loved to jump in piles of them, newly raked and red and gold and copper. I have always envied trees. I like trucks and vintage cars. I do not like the smell of new cars. But I do like the fruity car fresheners you get at the car wash. The ones you hang from your mirror. They make me feel like a kid. And a pimp. I loved music before I was even born. My mother played the piano the whole time she was pregnant with me. She played for the church choir. My father was the choir director. They were like a gospel Peaches and Herb. Because my parents were in charge of the music, we were always in church. But at least there we knew they couldn't fight.

We went to a tiny all black, Baptist church where people regularly got the spirit. Whenever that happened, the big-boned women dressed in white would rush to stand on either side of the spirited person to try to contain them, so they couldn't run up and down the aisles. The organ player usually tried to instigate once he knew people were getting excited. He would play faster so people would want to shout. The big-boned women would use the fans from the local funeral home to try and cool the spirit down. The big-boned women were a part of what was called the nurses guild. They always had peppermints, which they passed out like medicine. If you were fidgeting, one peppermint. If you got hungry, (which was inevitable because church could last long after the football games) two peppermints or maybe even a butterscotch. I later found out the big-boned women weren't really nurses. Just the wives of the deacons. I was disappointed. Why call them the nurses guild? I always wanted to get the spirit. It looked like fun. Instead I would get a headache.

My parents separated for the third and final time when I was nine. It was an ugly divorce. Fitting for a volatile marriage. Even still, I did not understand why they thought their lives should look different. I did not understand about dreams. And what happens when they don't come true. I took my dad's side. But I had to live with my mother. We moved into a house after she left my dad. My two older sisters, my mother and me. For me, this new house was a big deal. It was all ours. And I had a room of my own.

My mother loved to sing jazz standards like Nancy Wilson. She taught me how to play "Someone to Watch over Me" on the piano when I was ten. It was the first song I learned to play from beginning to end. Then she taught me "Don't Go to Strangers." On Saturday mornings when she thought we were asleep, she would sit downstairs and play those songs and also "Good Morning, Heartache" and "My Funny Valentine." I would tiptoe from my room to sit on the stairs. I would lean against the wall and imagine she was singing to me. I had never heard her sound so much like the truth. On Saturdays, she made me the most proud. She never knew I was listening.

But the other days of the week weren't like that. I didn't speak much. And my handwriting had gotten so small it was illegible. I used to close my eyes and concentrate really hard, trying to become invisible. It didn't work. But I eventually scared everyone enough that they called in my dad.

I went to live with him before I turned eleven. My mother gave me her piano when I was twelve. She was moving to California. It must have been hard for my dad to hear me play like her. But he would always ask me to. And he would point out where I wasn't as good. I started to hate playing. It was too much. And so I stopped.

My dad had to rely on his old records. He had hundreds of them, dusty and in stacks in the corner. From James Brown to James Taylor, Frank Sinatra to Frankie Lymon and the Teenagers, Earth, Wind and Fire to the *Four Seasons* by Vivaldi. We had a musical library in our living room worthy of the Smithsonian. He played his records every night, educating me on whoever we were listening to. And that was how I got to know my father. And eventually how I got to know myself.

Music became a haven for me. An escape. Music was a promise. It whispered to me. And taught me to dream. I would go to my room, turn off the lights, and turn on my music. I would lay on my bed, and listen. In memoriam for the end of a horrible day, in appreciation of a beautiful one, to know my feelings when I was too numb to find them on my own. I would listen. I still do that. Maybe you do that. Maybe you'll play one of my songs sometime when you do. And maybe you'll dream with my dreams in the background. And so for a moment, neither of us will be alone.

## JOHN TRAN
`Home Grown/Red Panda`

### *About Me:*

I've drank my own pee, shit my pants, seen most of the world, lied, told the truth, been on *Singled Out*, switchstance heelflip to noseslide, broke my wrist and collarbone and a head concussion from a 2ft jump snowboarding, got arrested for skateboarding, rode my bike into a basketball pole, traveled to and through the four corners of the United States of America which are Hawaii, Alaska, Maine, and Key West FL, pop shove-it late kickflip, been caught masturbating to porn by my mom, made friends, lost friends, made enemies, had sex with friends that became enemies, crashed my first car into a transit bus, fakie hardflip, jacked off with Ben-Gay, and had a top-10 hit in Hawaii. What the fuck have you done?

**BRENDAN BROWN**

## The Receiving End of Sirens

Of ritual and habit I opened my mouth
to find the prisoners inside had made their way out.

A verbal vestige where nouns once played
sits empty and lonely and still on my face.

Soon ended the clawing at my cheeks and gums,
as I searched in my molars for words but found none.

Within me a well of speech had run dry,
so I tried to siphon language from people nearby.

But nothing they said could seem to console
the fact that my mouth was naught but a hole.

## SCHUYLAR CROOM

### *Letter to a Gypsy*

Guard your comfort my dear, guard your heart,
as the sailor takes locks of hair,
and prisons a piece of cloth or picture.
The wealthy have overbought and undersold their memories.
Even if they duplicate your treasures,
they still will never love them
for the reasons you have learned to love them.

It's a painful mistake on her part,
to try and become someone just because that someone may
be happier,
prettier, truly more free.
But she will not learn that.
And out of everything you can give her, you cannot teach her
to love herself.

She is Midas in a world of unpolished gold.
And you are a goddess with no care for shiny things.
Be flattered my dear. Because your beautiful soul is sparkling
never the less.

And she sees it.
And can't stand that with all of her riches she can't by your
happiness.

I think you are the kindest soul I can't ever meet.
And if guarding your simple joys is the only wrong you are
doing
then I think you are more noble than I.

You deserve your treasures,
And a true gypsy would never let them out of sight.
I will give you a chest with lock and key.
And I will help you fill it with goodness.

If you don't want me to know where you have buried that, I
will respect that too.

Just remember that no money can buy a shovel long enough to
dig down into your heart.

Hell or high water my love.
You are so big in my world,

yours,
—Schuylar

**VINCENT REYES**

`Create!`

## *Lao-tzu and a Friend Play a Game of Marbles*

They danced all night to the sound
of bird beak and cedar wood.
In the morning they boiled green leaves
and shared a pot of honey for lunch.

They talked all day about wind and water.

They talked about the good manners man
may receive if he sits alone and quiet on a dead log
for three days straight.

At sunset they sat under a pine tree and played
an ancient game of glass marbles that goes
like this:

One sage strikes the yellow marble
with his fingernail in order to move
the other's crimson one.
The entire game is played in silence
for about a hundred years until the yellow
marble, the one with the sun inside,
hits the crimson one, the one with their blood.

Their glass shells eventually will shatter and two canaries
    one yellow,
    one crimson,
    and both with black beaks
will be revealed shortly before they all fly away.

## *Dalí*

"Strange fish, pulled by an invisible thread"
writes Leo Leonni to explain the science
of amphibious migration.

Today a humpback whale washed up on
a Spanish seaside.

Today a train derailed near Osaka killing seventy-one
and on this day a powerful flood took hundreds
of children away from their mother's grip
in the Pacific Islands

Tomorrow marine biologists may discover,
upon closer inspection of the washed up whale,
that it has waterproof pocket watches for eyes.

Maybe it will live,
Maybe we will live,

if you could call the sound of seconds
ticking the beginning of some sort of vital sign.

## MEG FRAMPTON
Meg & Dia

For the first time, this sickness is no mere natural invasion is no consequence of an ugly decision to let myself go for one . . . lonely . . . night is no punishment for indulgence of any particular pleasure

This sickness is my price I pay for the submission of my life to a promise.

For the first time A must be A. I must believe and rely on this factor with nothing more than my tottering judgment.

The weight accumulated on my mind is worth conjuring the impossible. The fatigue gathering in my spine is a bargain!

To wake each morning becomes more and more difficult but it doesn't matter . . . not much.

There is no pre-destiny and if all this is some sick accident I am forever indebted to free will and cause and effect for allowing me a chance to be sick. A sad, sorry product of the twenty-first century. Swept along with the masses in one huge hypnotic festival. I refuse. Refuse!

Which is why I choose to be sick . . .

If there is no cure, no medicine, I hope in the end all the pretty pictures will make sense, and at least to some, itchy Picasso merges into the finality and solid defiance of Da Vinci.

"Oh, I see! She breathes!" they'll say in wonder . . .

and that, dear sir, is all I ever wanted them to say.

**DIA FRAMPTON**

## *Hospitals Always Smell Like Decaying Hair*

I waited outside for almost twelve hours. I kept thinking of everything I wanted to tell you . . . dear best friend.

It had been over a year since we had known your future. You dropped your interest in horoscopes, while I still desperately searched both of ours to see if they would end up running parallel. I still needed a palm reader, while you quietly and politely asked for more pain reliever.

Sure darling, and a cup of water, too.

They wouldn't let me see you. How could I ask for any compassion anyways. They cared more about seeing their secretaries or patients in sedatives then their own wives.

2 p.m.

2:01 p.m.

"Yes, please. No sugar. Black. Decaf."

2:02 p.m.

There was a funny purple stain on the carpet next to the fish tank.

2:03 p.m.

You're dead.

I stand up. I didn't take the cup from the lady in white. Her unnaturally stretched face looked concerned, but her overly extended eyebrows were pulled so unevenly that it failed to give her any real sympathetic look. You were an angel in pale blood and struggling skin, while she was already a corpse to me.

My neck hurt from sitting so long. You would have apologized about the wait if you would have woken up and walked through those doors: an ugly angel in an old grey T-shirt, escorted by bastards from Harvard in white, needles protruding from the angles of their hands.

Well, it turns out I waited for nothing.

You never came.

Outside it was sterile and dry. The clouds seemed to shift slowly over my head as I walked toward Fifth Avenue. They looked like giant fingers of bedsheets on blue, kinda how your eyes looked only in winter when your skin was a light silver. I had known this outcome and I had prepared for it, thank God.

I lit a Parliament, my last one, and began to blow strings of smoke into the air slowly.

I saw your neighbor five doors down, standing in a huge red dress, watering her plants on the side of her walkway.

She stopped when she saw me, inquired curiously, and I told her the news.

She started to cry.

I knew she cared more about her fucking garden than you. Somehow she got it engraved in her head that it was a sin not to cry at the death of a person much younger. It was proper for a God-fearing Catholic to cry at a death.

What a sorry piece of shit she was.

I felt more apathetic for her than I did you.

I know you would have, too.

I went inside and poured a scotch and water like my old friend Cho from Japan had shown me. The water settled on the top until I mixed it with my bloody nails.

Had I really been that anxious?

## JOSH PARTINGTON
`Firescape/Something Corporate`

### *27 Hours*

These pieces of conversation have
left me dry and hungry
for tethered remains and

catalytic addictions that I can never hope to shake.

I've been up for 27 hours
the only hope I have in me now
is that I can make it to 30
without having to talk to someone I really care about.

The depravity in my sleep
acts more like a hangover
and at this rate I could be pretty drunk
by the time my eyes close.

I hear everything.
Every whisper in my house is adjacent to my eardrum.
I hear the people sleeping in my living room
and I can hear their dreams
and want to make them mine.
I want so bad to be in a rested head.
Tomorrow is now today and yesterday seems like last week.
Take a hit . . . it might last longer this time.

## *Orchids*

There was a brilliant white orchid
living on the first floor
of the Chaparral Heights apartment complex.
She was my lonely, beautiful neighbor
that bloomed every fall, and
conspicuously, wilted by spring: no one knew
where she spent her summers. No one asked.

In later years, the orchid
grew vibrant, as if becoming
a woman of distinction.

Now, it is March, and I could not miss her more.

## JARED DRAUGHON
`Classic Case`

### *New York City Vampires*

Smell the flowers,
Wine and dine,

It's so beautiful to decide.
You don't have to tell me twice,

I'm not taking your advice at all.
At the door there's a knock,
Sudden loss of blood leads to shock.

Now my wish is your command,
Your presence is in demand,
And I feel obliged to shut my eyes and make that wish again.

Call it quits,
Off to bed,
You should stop while you are ahead.

You're not reaping what you sow,
Because it's all in who you know.
Ignorance is bliss unless you wish to know the truth and live.

You're an empty heart.

---

### Human Error

Some say the glass is half full,
Some say that it's half empty.

We should trust machines to make up our minds.
Human error keeps us guessing all our lives.
Trust in machines they will keep us alive.

Some say we came from Eden,
Some say we all are primates.

We should trust machines to make up our minds.
Human error keeps us guessing all our lives.

Trust in machines they will keep us alive.
Some say the end is coming,
Some say that we're just starting.

We should trust machines to make up our minds.
Human error keeps us guessing all our lives
Trust in machines they will keep us alive.

**COLLEEN NAPOLITANO**

## The Study

Well the kids stare at the history books
and listen, half-aware, to learn
that the world of Picasso, Da Vinci, Thoreau
is dead.
It seems the creators were destroyed
by some meteor or an ice age in the airwaves.
You can see what they left behind, the artifacts—
their fossilized bones hang, under a light blanket of
dust, in any museum [some carelessly loiter
on shelves with yellowed pages falling out].
Where have all the artists gone?
They must've sold their hearts
for a less complicated reality.
Or became the soldiers in a war against—what was it again?—
something they can't quite recall.
Charcoal faces with lines blurring
into the creases, stating boldly,
"I Want YOU to Give Up Now."
And there are those who claim,
with sneering arrogance,
that they never really existed at all.
In such a static age, who do you believe?

And now there is a new breed, the common
"Bukowski-wannabe."
Who lingers around coffee shops and quiet cafes sullenly,
with the life completely drawn out of their face,
asking for a fresh cup, "something strong and black as my
    soul . . .
if I had one."
On the cracking pale porcelain, they leave their fossils,
two red bent ellipses of cheap lipstick and words just as cheap,
just waiting to be washed away.

**RICH BALLING**
The Sound of Animals Fighting

*Einstein on the Beach*

Philip Glass must have reinvented the larynx
when he reinvented the opera.

	Five successive hours of calculated cunning
(if only I had such power over women).

A survivor of both John Adams and
Thomas Ades . . .

but never, Mr. Glass, have I heard such
penetrating arpeggios as these.

## Werner Herzog

I am the artist coveted by most.
Fellini never thought it would be me.
Behind the single malt or shot of gin

the film apprentice might consume to be
a fraction of what I have done for them,
I am the artist coveted by most.

In jungles I lay days and nights with death.
Disease and Kinski gnawing at each nerve.
Behind the single malt or shot of gin

that Bergman's ever drunk since *Nosferatu*,
or *Fitzcarraldo* or *The Wrath of God,*
I am the artist coveted by most . . .

by Wong Kar-Wai and even David Lynch.
Guerilla in the midst of German film
Behind the single malt or shot of gin.

It's cinema or cinnamon today:
a fresh perspective is few and far between.
I am the artist coveted by most
Behind the single malt or shot of gin.

## Sarah Kane

if any play could earn the terza rima
that Dante found so eloquently fit,
propose a work from Sarah Kane's brief canon

like *Blasted, Crave,* or *Phaedra's Love* or *Skin.*
a playwright passed down from the Gods themselves
whose Godliness brought her to bitter end.

and now we watch the scholars fill their shelves:
*4.48 Psychosis, Cleansed* and then
what would have come i'll not attempt to tell,

the work she chose to give us is enough.
the freshest words since Charles I've befell,
i'm sure he would have even liked her stuff.

Camus, Bukowski, Beckett, John L'Heureux
the next, Sarah, addition, here, is you.

## H. P. Lovecraft

A private hospital for the insane
*He bore the name of Charles Dexter Ward*
An antiquarian from infancy
The pits whose inhuman cadences rose
had drawn down nameless horrors from the skies

## *Calvino*

If on a winter's night a traveler
Perhaps you started leafing through the book
If on a winter's night a traveler
Perhaps you started leafing through the book
This sentence sounds somehow familiar

## *Celine*

The lady lies down in a mess of lace
It lingers on in the smell of her death
"Ah!" she says "It's burst." She meant her abscess
It pounded worse than forty-nine truck horses
Enormous mounds all tangled up like bushes

## JASON GLEASON
`ActionReaction`

### For the Day

Call to me oh, Cannibal,
When the heavy work is done.
Call to me a liar, & a beggar, & a son.
Call an angry officer,
Un-televised, Unsung.
Call to me the serpent's Tongue,
To tell me I am young.

Call to me a roof maker.
Some rain is leaking in,
Past my fear, and past my Courage
To the puddle in my brain.

Call to me my bedroom floor
To see it all undone
And my cupboards are all empty
Except for One

For The Day, the sun will rise.
And for tonight, my sorry eyes
Can see the Reason that we call it,
Masquerade.

### *It May as Well Have Been March 21, 1982.*

(three random thoughts)

thought #1

Meanwhile,
As I go.
I often end up wondering. Lately,
As if by sudden force,
I would lie in submission to my day. (or life, for that matter)

For Time, is irrelative. Or $\Sigma$
Relatively.
Irrelevant to any western Thought.
Or so I think.
And I keep on thinking. Lately,
As if by a great, sudden force,
That I would ever lie down.
To face the dirt.
And so on.
And sometimes.
And so forth.

thought #2

Where did all the believers go?
The ones who tell the dreamers, they're Alive.
We need an army! Believers with desire damnit!
And not those pansies that make believe.
Just the ones who
      Know
          That
      LOVE
Will Cure.

I will test the Chameleons of Sleep,
And the Believers will sort them,
And I truly believe that.

thought #3

This one's gonna be long winded,
So stop now if you're not even going to bother.

### If Humans Have Heartbeats, Do Robots Have Heartbeeps?

Catch my sleepy head,
Carry it down a long way.
Watch my field of view,
And carry it down a long way
How bright the souls of heaven, and dull that wander home.
When the Lord is done with me,
He will.
If we can lift the wheel, we will.
If they can sew it up, they will.
Catch my sleepy head, and carry it down a long way.

Breed, you summer girls,
Carry us on for long days.
Feed us when we forget to feed,
To carry us on for long days.
If one contests your place in Heaven,
My Hand will strike him down. Then you will see.
When the Lord is done with me,
He will.
If we can break the doors, we will.
If they can bring us to rest, they will.
So, Breed you summer girls, To carry us on for long days.

When will we see the day
of death without morning?
Green skies above the water
& Light below.
The day we all become
One simple thought of noise.
In a vast open Mind.
As if we weren't the very moment we were seen.
Sun drenched & Naked,
But not alone
If I can lift the wheel, I will.
If I can sew it up, I will.
Catch my sleepy head, and carry it down the long way.

## ALEXANDER KENT
Say Anything

### A Short Clip from "The Unlikeliness of Counterpane"

Characters:

Spudnik Arugala Rhubarb

Wealthy, an eye for success, this 6th grade boy plays 2nd string attack on the lacrosse team. Although most boys this age have no clue, Spudnik does not know who he is and tends to believe he has a co-existing, ever-changing, alternate mind.

Genivive

Witty, modest yet aggressive, she loves to volunteer at senior citizen centers. She knows her shit.

Joebob Ralph Lauren

Loves his name. He's tall, an early bloomer and can relax you until you forget about homework.

"I had the craziest day, guys . . . I mean, CRAZY!"
exclaimed Spudnik, looking up at the long-sleeve sky.
Genivive and Joebob couldn't help but not move or
gesture towards Spudnik to let him know that they were
interested. They were entranced by the wool sky and
the stars its mother had sewn into it.

Joebob moved only his lips, "Tell us about it jonnnnny."

Spudnik then, half regrettingly, opened his mouth. "Well, I woke up at around 11:30, slept through my 9:45 alarm. I sat down to pee, as I enjoyed in times of no rush, and got a call from Chris. He asked me if I still wanted to go to Guitar Center. You see, I was looking for a microphone for my Midi Keyboard. Realizing it was Tuesday, I checked movie times and asked Annie if she wanted to see a 5 dollar movie, our Tuesday habitual. We decided on *Proof* at 5:30 and I began the day. Same thing as the night before, a Burberry-scented black long-sleeve, some fruit-stained Lucky jeans and my penguin Vans were thrown on in a rush. I conscientiously turned out the lights and ran out my door. After this I drove to my dad's house where I infiltrated his garage and got my Harry Potter books, a 22" ride cymbal to lend to Marc and my Gnome Checkers (unopened). I rushed to Brian's house where I encountered him and Ryan. We unloaded my bass amp and the ride cymbal. Chris moseyed on over, unshaven, with sunglasses on. He looked like a relaxed drug lord, to be honest. I stood there, by the garage door, dumbfounded. I WASN'T SUPPOSED TO BE THERE! I was supposed to be behind the drum set! I ran over behind the wooden contraption as quickly as possible and instantaneously picked up the sticks. Then me and some all stars rip-rop-rooted the place into shambles.

I got four blisters. Next thing I knew I was
convincing Ryan that broccoli cheddar soup = uber. He
believed but didn't like it mucho. We got to guitar
center and I didn't find any cool mics. I walked
across the street, paid my own cellular telephone
bill, BY AUTOMATED MACHINE, and drove back west. The
drive was short. I picked up Annie and we went to
Coffee Bean to get our favorite little fixes. LARGE
pure chocolate with soy milk and a LARRRRGE double
vanilla tea latte. For some reason, I had this
uber-obsession with vanilla. Annie's friend LoLo
called me and asked me where we were. (She was rendez
vous-swa-zeeee-ing us at the movie theater.)
"'Hey where are you guys?'
"'We're across the street at the Beanery'
"'OK'
"'We'll be there soon'
"'OK'
"We walked into the movie theater and saw 48 people
over the age of 65 or so. That made the movie's total
attendance so far 51. After the movie I peed in a
stall where I miraculously recollected thoughts I had
created in that very same, unrecognizable poop coop.
Even better, the thoughts I recollected were confident
aspirations of becoming a ninja. Then my beautiful
lovely sweetheart cupcake dollface offered an
adventure to the beach—with tea! More vanilla tea,
socks and shoes off later, we were waltzing down the
dance floored beach. Hand in hand, lip to lip, eye to

eye, BRAIN TO BRAIN. We talked about the tattoos of power animals we were going to get in 10 or so days, her 18th birthday coming up soon (that very Sunday), and COLLEGE. She told me she would enjoy Florida if I wanted to go, and that it would be EASIER on our growth. I love her. So many thoughts in my head. Do I quit my band? I mean, my life is dependent upon this amazing yet crazy person, but that seemed like a whole different story.

"I took Annie home, and called Chris. He was at Rico's and I asked him to get me a burrito and invited him and the all stars over to my house. They came, they saw, they left. We got high, and Marc, Chris, and I went to Blockbuster where I bought a lovely bunch of DVDs. Then me, Marc, Ryan, Chris, Gabe, and Brian all watched a movie in my room. I lathered my body in honey milk and rode on into the night."

"All you needed were some cool waves, a tasty buzz, and you were fine," rumbled Joebob.
"Ha." They all laughed in unison.
"Are you still high Mr. Rhubarb? YER IN SIXTH GRADE!
. . . I saw you in Mrs. Kronemeyer's class earlier . . .
Asked you if I could borrow a pencil? We walked down to Honor's Pre Algebra together, holding hands to be controversial.
You've never played an instrument, let alone go to a guitar center, or had a cell phone! WAKE UP SPUD!"

Spudnik turned to his right. He stared Genivive in the eye, and she knew not to speak. He turned to his left and did the same with Joebob. He started articulating a word, but stopped 1/2 a syllable into it. Genivive busted first, she always did. She could never hold her laughter in for more than 4.8 seconds. It would be written in the history books someday.

"It must have been a daydream. But it seemed so real. I mean, I feel like I WAS THIS GUY. Is that a memory from the future or is it the mescaline we did earlier laced with weed?"

"The latter," Genivive stated relaxingly.
"I don't know what that means, bitch!" Joebob cried, offended.

Genivive was a smarty pants, she loved showing the guys up.


To be continued . . .

## JARROD TAYLOR
`In Reverent Fear`

### *A Young Mother's Medicine*

Oh Lord, how I want to fall in love in ease by the lake in
St. James.
With smoke in the evening sun, I will sleep and I won't move

Oh Lord what am I to do with me, my mind falling off the
hazel trees?
I go from wanting graciously to not at all.

A young mother's medicine is strange.

Oh mother, I want to be a child before all the salting came
in me.
To love not as a boy with almond skin, but ripe as an apple's
skin I'll love

A young mothers medicine is stranger than you thought;

1 part paranoia
2 parts bread and wine
1/2 a cup of sugar
and any drug you find

I'm wasted all the afternoons

I never sleep at all
My heart's a famine murdered land
I dare not speak of God.

And it's strange, but I wish I could fall in it.

I wish I would.

**BEN JORGENSEN**

### *The Big Reveal*

It's the big reveal.
All the people standing around you a second ago were just
actors in your life.
Now they're clapping and laughing and walking over to you.

You figured it out.
Ten thousand dollars cash.
Paid vacation to Bermuda.
It was all just a game.
Nothing was ever as bad as you thought.
A test for some reality TV show.

**RICH PALMER**

`Buddhah`

## *Do What You Need to Be Happy*

I was chasing Ewoks on a motorcycle today. It was such a sight to see their furry firm rumps bounding side to side with each gallop of their cute little padded bear feet. They screamed in gloriously choired beeps and pulses as I revved my gilded stallion faster and harder into the frantic mass of bear dolls. Some hid behind garbage cans and fire hydrants; some ran into houses through cat doors and peeked out through cracked venetian blinds as I continued to chase down their friends.

For some of the heavier ones, the thrill of fast sport was too much in the sullen mid-July sun, and they collapsed on the pavement.

Some of the fallen I would swerve not to hit.

Others I would aim for.

The cute ones, I would swing a rusty crowbar toward the crowns of their skulls. Clipping bloody bone fragments into parked car doors and pedestrians, a fan of blood and fur would often erupt from these departed playthings, while an etching of matted hair would stretch the concrete as I rode on after the last visible Ewok, huffing and dragging its sorry battered soul into an abandoned alleyway for safe haven.

I dismounted my gnarly steed and crept slowly up to the alley delta.

"It's only Luke, your old friend, don't be sad about the others, I want to help you little man," I soothed, palms outstretched, on my knees in the alley opening.

With an uncertain rustling, the hairy ball appeared from out of his Dumpster hideout. Its gleaming eyes projected a light blue beyond ethical description, and an ecstasy of purity and innocence seemed to glorify and define a race of immeasurable serenity.

I got up as the Ewok bumbled toward me with little furry feet and wrinkled hands collaborating in a tattered waltz of contentment.

When the creature was about two feet in front of me, I reached into my back pocket, grabbed and cocked my P228 police-issued, loaded handgun and unwound a single bullet straight through the front of its face and out the back, sending the stunted round skipping along down the alleyway.

With a sudden slump, the delicate creature collided with the ground by my feet, splattering fur and crimson on my boots and jeans. Its big blue eyes glazed erect and straight into the sun. I turned and walked back to my bike, and drove to the nearest Dunkin' Donuts for some coffee and an éclair.

## PORTER McKNIGHT
`Atreyu`

Come tell me old man,
Whilst I am bathing in our wounded,
ankle-deep in what remains of family
Why do we fight this war?
For fame?
Or fortune?
Here I see my brothers,
White faced, lying still beside me,
I feel contempt for what you've brought us.

The ground here is like a morbid canvas.
Necks contorted in fashions the mind could never comprehend.
Wasted frames of men.
Sinking.
Wallowing.
Writhing in perforated agony.
Cleanse us of this offense!
This sickening excuse for glory.
(A feeling arises deep in his breast)
The world goes dark

I cannot refuse death in this moment.
This all can end!
This all could save us.

O sweet death, deliver us from evil!
This is suffering of another level.
Bring mercy to my pitiful name.

Rise.
(The firmament isn't ready for you.)

The stench of death is not easy to portray.
I wished for an Apocalypse.
I'm surrounded by a catacomb.
Where are the others?
No spectator in sight.
Just revengeful calm.
Look at what has become of our feud.

Bravery, in this circumstance, takes many forms.
Grace granted by the loss of a single soul.
One whose name is now set free.
An overwhelming stress lifted from his chest.
Their violence is a legend told in every land.

## KIRK HUFFMAN
### Gatsbys American Dream

My apartment was muggy when I awoke.
The ceiling at first blurred until its white-dulled-yellow
smoke-stained
color bloomed into focus.
Shit that sunrise is bright.
Maybe I will open a window.
At first it was the chirping of birds, the rustling of the fresh
green ivy
in the breeze which had slowly conquered the old brick red
of the antique hotel.
All of it flowing in front of an awe-inspiring blue.
Slowly.
I admired it with all five senses.
"You're about to see some kung-fu shit, like you ain't ever
fuckin' seen"
bam.
Hello. Do you know where you are, Stan?
your garden of eden.
9:48am
dante's inferno.
fucking junkies.
starbucks parking lots
jake whoops on by and engine pistons roar the commuting
swarm car alarms

7 story condo buildings featuring studios, 1 and 2 bedrooms
with 9,500 square feet of street-level retail space

my apartment was muggy when I laid back down and lit up a
smoke

**ALEX HOVIS**
Paper Models

## *Never Forget Her*

Models, stacks of magazines
Read between the lines of speed
We can't trail, move so slow anymore
The way she wore neckties, and her crack eyes
The Xenadrine, she does it for me

Get excited, not today
Show emotion, not today
Warm Vanilla Sugar lingers on my sheets
Your green eyes, your real brown eyes
Endless late drives, oh how hard I tried

Drink yourself into a mess
We do what we wish for best
I'll keep you up all night without your consent
Out your window is the road we'll never know
Your bedroom door, though, it remains closed

You'll never, never forget her
But sooner or later you'll wish you never met her
And I'll warn you but you'll soon only regret her

**GRETA SALPETER**

The Hush Sound

## *You are the moon*

Shadows all around you as you surface from the dark,
Emerging from the gentle grip of night's unfolding arms
Darkness, darkness everywhere, do you feel all alone?
The subtle grace of gravity, the heavy weight of stone

You cannot see what you possess, a beauty calm and clear
That floods the sky and blurs the darkness like a chandelier
All the light that you possess is skewed by lakes and seas,
The shattered surface, so imperfect, is all that you believe

I want to bring a mirror, so silver and correct
So precise and so pristine, a perfect pane of glass
I will set the mirror up to face the blackened sky
So you will see your beauty every moment that you rise.

## New Year's Eve

Green bottles glow on the floor
Scattered around a warm bed,
Your silhouette is soft on the edges.
Let's fill the bottles with all of our worried words;
We'll throw them in the cold, dark lake
And follow our breath as we walk home.

**ROB MORRIS**

`The Hush Sound`

*the mess i've made for you*

Please use cup holders.

Click . . .

A camera is never around when you need one for that perfect
shot . . .
A 6, and a 5, and a 7, ate, 9, in a deck scattered at who knows
what time . . .
Casino's time flies by and no one notices the minute hands
devouring brain cells . . .
Half-empty glasses are full at the bottom with condensation
rings on the table . . .

Leaving traces . . . memories . . . anything . . .

Fall is here again and the bottles are almost all empty
The truth is in the air like cheap whiskey.

Click . . .

A little piece of you is staying with me,
A little piece of you is within this photograph,
A little piece of you is coming with me,

Like it or not . . .

A little piece of you still cares.

The decks missing cards in a game made for pairs.
All the same suit . . . no suitors . . .

Click . . .

I ran for a pen to draw you a map . . . Of the fastest way home tonight.
I'll dot all the tollways, dash all the freeways . . . And shade every mountain range for you

Color me caring . . .
With contrasts of regrets . . . on the darker faces . . .
All face cards but no queen.

Put on my poker face and never show you the hand that hides my face . . .
The joker I once was is shuffled and lost in figures and odds . . .

Click . . .

Kiss goodnight . . . while I know they're looking at my cards . . .
The house always wins . . . I act so well like I don't mind . . .

It's just fun . . . It's just a kiss . . . It's just a moment that I won't miss . . .

You've got a 15-hour drive . . . with some plain states ahead and you're tired.
But I don't offer lodgings . . . my house always wins . . .
no I don't offer comfort in the coldest shoulders I impose on you.

Say cheese honey . . . then hit the road . . .

Click . . .

### the sinking of some great ship

Quiet! A heart speaks out, can you hear it?
Quick! Stethoscope, scalpel, hurry damnit.

"What's it saying?"
"It's flopping around."

Myocardial infarction. Heart attack
Lung sounds breathing agonal respirations
Last breaths escaping in such a common manner
Blood cells crying,

"Are you a doctor?"
"You're hurting me like they all did."

Speaking out against the madman in the spoon.
"Do you feel safe here?"
"Our safes empty and ravaged."

"Thanks to you . . . I'm here . . .
Without a penny in my pocket I would still hold you
When you're shaking, screaming, and turning blue"

Sterilized for your lack of protection.

"Is it because of lack of attention? Affection?"

On the table surrounded you're getting all you need and then some.
Were confused on what a "last time" really means.
We've heard it so many times lately.

Fighting four on one to keep you in the basement
Dotted arms like tiny chicken pox on your forearms
Squeeze through the crack as we try to close the door
The tears in our eyes could have filled riverbanks to flood levels

I can't help it . . . I've got a temper . . . I can't lose it . . .

"Sit down shut up, because the last straw has been drawn, and my temper is at its shortest right now, so please stop trampling my heart."

## SCOTT WALDMAN
The City Drive

## *Is Bette Midler a True Star?*

Is Bette Midler a true star?
Nah.
Stars shine in the sky.
Bette Midler ain't no star.
Polaris, now that's a star!

**DANNY SMITH**

The City Drive

## *Hesperia*

Tell me what it's like
Living under lights
And stares
From coffeepots
And secondhand newsprint
I'm listening
Tell me what you like
I'll shut off the lights
Downstairs
There's a Carpenter
She's singing her heart out
We're listening

And lucky stars are counted
Lucky stars are counted
In Hesperia tonight

Daughters grow up fast
She's the smartest in her class
She says, "Wake up!
It's suppertime!"
(shepherd's pie. Heather's new recipe)

Donuts for dessert
Uncle Wiggly skips a turn
I lose
I hang my head
Cheryl says, "Let's go to bed"
Sounds good to me

And lucky stars are counted
Lucky stars are counted
In Hesperia tonight

**TRAVIS BRYANT**
Goodbye Tomorrow

## save the boy

i had to do something with the loose ends
so i tied them around my legs
i saw patience in the water as i gazed in
deserving so much less

as i sank the noise and colors left my head
in perfect clarity i'd missed
nineteen years old when numb killed cold
forever

i wasnt gasping so tell them when theyre asking
tell them what i said
there was nothing i could do with the things left to prove
so i gave up on them

i couldnt save the boy who used to feel alive
the boy who had his mother's smile
he used to swim but we're losing him
to the current

## *missouri*

can you tell me
about missouri
about the weather
on the drive
was it raining
in missouri
windshield blurring
when you arrived
did you drink enough
not to worry
or feel sorry
for the child
you were leaving
with nothing
and no one and nowhere
just eighteen years of life

that youre sorry doesnt make a damn thing right
no good intentions will ever change her life
that you fear the dark doesnt mean you love the light
i never thought missouri would be the reason that i cry

is it worth mentioning
that she had a sibling
that hasnt been clean

for a day in his life
hes been popping pills
and brawling men
in every state from texas up to washington
do you blame yourself
think of someone else
is it taking all you have to stay alive
is their grace for men
or only consequence
are you prepared to bear them for everyone
you cheated in this life

that youre sorry doesnt make a damn thing right
no good intentions will ever change her life
that you fear the dark doesnt mean you love the light
i never thought missouri would be the reason that i cried

i finally see
why she believes in me
never having the luxury
of affording dreams
or chasing them
to all the places i have been
the seas of faces through which i swim
on my way

## AARON CHAPMAN
### Nurses

I spoke with GOD last night, and being the benevolent being that he is, he had some surprisingly keen insight he'd like me to pass on. GOD said he would like the word and notion "god" to be replaced with the word "life."
That it should be worshipped as wholeheartedly as he was.
GOD went on to say all the idolization was beginning to make him feel a tad "big headed" and that worshipping existence would make him just as happy.
GOD thought it would be a good idea for people to take an hour (or 5) out of each Sunday to go somewhere new and appreciate anything at all. GOD also thought it wise to brush up on science (or another field of interest) in that time. GOD mentioned that doing service or just being really nice would suffice as well.
In LIFEism:
<u>All donations</u> are to be researched contributions to a worthy charity or to the community in which you live.
<u>Sins</u> are completely relative to environment and genetics, and are to be taken up with your fellow man. Repentance likewise.
<u>Clergy</u> will be self-appointed mentors that know anything you don't.
The only commandments are:
1. Be a good person as best you can. All cases are relative to the individual 2. Live as much life as you can 3. Pursue something

you deem worthy of your time in your relatively short amount
on earth.
4. Love all

GOD's last words were: "Have all the ladies put 'em on the
glass!"

**DAMON DAW**

Nurses

## *Musicalism*

The sad state of the music industry today can be attributed to one thing and one thing alone: it has in fact ceased to be an "industry" and has become a "business." An industry differs from a business in that it is a system involved in producing and marketing tools to the public that aim to maximize the standard of living of those that purchase and implement them. One might say that an industry is concerned with the creation and distribution of technologies, music being one of these. A business, on the other hand, is an organization whose primary concern is selling products at a maximum net profit with lowest overhead costs, while placing a secondary emphasis on the impact of the product on the lives of consumers. Present-day companies that finance bands and individual performers (primarily, but not limited to, "major labels") have effectively changed most mainstream music from a tool of technology, to a product.

While the realm of popular thought usually labels tools that have come into existence only through modern scientific research and innovation as technology, I believe it is almost certain, beyond any doubt, that early humans used experimental trial-and-error methods to discover, improve, and eventually utilize music as an extremely powerful psychotropic, technological tool. As such, the discovery of music, similar to the invention of language, was so instinctual and ancient that it has not been popularly recognized as having fundamental scientific origins and technological implementations.

Organizations that constitute the modern music business have made the transition from technological supply entities to profit-acquiring entities efficiently and covertly by employing a variety of circular, self-sustaining marketing and manipulation methods. They know, as all good business people do, that the largest demographic with the largest disposable income will be the most desirable group to market any nonessential product to. It just so happens that in America and most of the world, young children and teenagers living with their parents constitute most of this demographic. It also turns out that this group's opinions and, correspondingly, their purchasing choices are easily manipulated. Music businesses prey on the universally image-conscious, status-seeking teenagers of the world by employing psychologically coercive advertising tools that convince them that to gain status with their peers they must purchase and use certain products. Once a specific musical trend is established by corporate advertising, it is easily exploited and maintained as specific products saturate the market. The need for further aggressive advertising is radically reduced at this point and the growing word-of-mouth persuasion will most likely sustain the trend until another kills and replaces it. The use of social pressure to sell products effectively removes most freedom that consumers may have had regarding what music to listen to and correspondingly limits the ability of the consumer to maximize the positive impact of music on their lives.

Profit mongering in the music business is accompanied by several destructive processes, maybe the most dangerous of which is the manufacturing and rewarding of unoriginality. Substantial creative progress will never be made in today's mainstream music environment because it is a business and businesses are not sustained by creative innovation but by the manufacturing of shallow gimmickry. It is not so much that popular music lacks complete creative merit, but it has been so overspecialized and filtered to fit current market trends that diversity has been almost completely eradicated.

Art has been and always will be an action of instinct and will. When individualism is abandoned for popular opinion we are robbed not only of our sincerity but our power, style, and soul.

**KENNY VASOLI**

`The Starting Line`

## *My Flaws Get Along*

I don't love the way I feel all of the time, but I don't feel the need for a billboard bullet or a bursting wallet with green coming out at the seams. I don't have care in a world that is fair, but that world is one I have never seen. My perfect skin is never coming in, but my scars all seem grown like a newborn son who just turned one at twenty-two years old. My love is strong when it gets along with the target that it's focused on, but my temper is short like when I was four when nothing was actually wrong. I take to heart things I should not, when thrown around in a casual talk. I put myself in an awkward place with a porcupine with a pretty face that I do try to kiss until it hurts my lips or one of us remains. I take in stride the flaws I hide from my blind side and camera eyes, but they reside with a smile so wide . . . they're live hermits that party all night.

## ELGIN JAMES
### Dream Weaver

I was eight years old when the Ku Klux Klan came to my town, and I couldn't help but take it personally. Being the only brown person within a seventy-mile radius, I had to ask myself who else could be responsible for the "black scourge" their pamphlets railed against. The Lawson twins? Asian sisters whose white father had adopted and brought them home after his tour in Vietnam, the girls still clutching each other and crying every time a low flying plane buzzed over recess? Or maybe the Giovanni family, Italians who owned Morris Town Pizza and only looked dark in the summer months? No, I knew I was to blame, and the "mongrels attacking the core of white society" were my hippie parents with their rainbow of adopted children.

Ironically, my parents came from bloodlines any racist would have been proud of. My father's family had grown fat on the Louisiana slave trade until the Southern defeat in the Civil War threw them into a poverty that persists to this day. As recently as World War II, my father's uncle (a member of the American Nazi Party) proudly flew a bloodred flag with a centered black swastika above his small neighborhood grocery store. The flag only flew for a few hours, though, before that same neighborhood burned the store to the ground.

On my mother's side, the family tree traces back to Houston Stewart Chamberlain, the purported Godfather of Eugenics, a ramshackle theory that some believe proves the Aryan race superior over all others. On the same branch of that tree is world famous Richard Wagner, whom Adolf Hitler himself declared the national composer of Nazi Germany.

Unfortunately, my unruly Afro and complexion betrayed my racial pedigree, because unlike the Giovanni family, I was cocoa-colored year round.

Family history may have played a part in launching my parents so aggressively into the civil rights movement. A shame that spurred them to march through the South, arms linked tight with blacks while dogs and high-powered hoses were set upon them. Why they continued in the struggle even after my father's friend James Chaney was murdered along with two whites by the Klan on a Southern dirt road (dramatized in the movie *Mississippi Burning*). And why my father chose to become a white pastor in an all black parish.

He'd tell us the story of a Sunday morning when members of the KKK surrounded the church, trapping the parishioners inside. The husband of the organist was late and pulled up to see thirty or so cloaked Klansmen armed with torches and shotguns. Worried for his wife he jumped out of his car and sprinted for the church. He almost made it. They got him about fifteen feet from the door. They dragged him to the back of a pickup truck and spread his limbs apart. A young man with a mouthful of tobacco cocked a Louisville slugger back on his shoulder like Mickey Mantle and then swung it down between the man's outstretched legs. The parish hugged and held back his hysterical wife while the Klan beat her husband. The cops (who my father assumed were under those white sheets) never showed.

I was raised on stories like this, so you can imagine why, after racist pamphlets found their way littered about our small town and the six o'clock news showed men in terrifying white hoods marching just twelve miles away in the city of Torrington, I spent the summer of my eighth year sleeping at the foot of my mother's bed.

We couldn't afford day care, and my older sisters were spending the summer at camp so my mom would bring me with her to the factory in Torrington. She'd let me stay in the car to listen to the radio while she worked her shift. I'd flip through the stations hoping for a gem like "Sometimes When We Touch" by Dan Hill or "Dream Weaver" by Gary Wright. I loved the anticipation as I searched through the static never knowing what I would find. I could spend hours like that and did, the eight hours of my mom's workday.

All that summer, though, I had been plagued by nightmares. I would be in the factory parking lot in the front seat of our station wagon when I would hear footsteps marching. I'd look in the rearview mirror and see a thousand Klansmen draped in white, their eyes black behind cut-out holes. I would start shaking, my small hands fumbling to open the car door. I'd want to run to the safety of the factory but I could never work the handle and the Klansmen would set upon the car, rocking it back and forth, breaking the windows, their hands reaching in to drag me out.

I would jolt awake in my bed choking on a scream stuck in the pit of my stomach. When my mother's alarm would buzz she'd find me curled up in my sleeping bag on her floor, because the soft sound of her breathing was the only thing that could lull me back to sleep.

I never told her about the dreams. She was spending more and more time crying when she thought I couldn't hear. Sobs hidden behind the bathroom door, eyes wet while she stood over the stove, her bedroom locked and dark in the afternoon ignoring my tentative knocks. That's why I never told her how hard third grade had been that year. How the kids at school called me nigger. How every time I got off the school bus the same rusted blue pickup truck was parked with its engine running. From the driver's seat eighteen-year-old Keith Kelly would spit a spray of tobacco juice on me, followed by whatever garbage happened to be in his truck. The veins in his neck and forehead bulging, he'd scream, "You fucking nigger, go the fuck home!" Which is exactly what I was trying to do except I figured he probably meant Africa.

Keith had bragged all over town about how he had joined the Knights of the Ku Klux Klan on his eighteenth birthday and the sudden appearance of "White Pride" pamphlets and "nigers (sic) out!" spray painted behind the town hall were widely assumed to be his handiwork.

I would walk as quickly as I could waiting for a half full can of Dr Pepper or a crumpled McDonald's bag to ricochet off the back of my head. I'd keep my eyes leveled on Bubba, my Chester White pig, waiting across the street. Smarter than any dog and just as loyal, he'd meet me at the end of our property every day after school. I'd crouch down, giving him a kiss on his pink snout and wait for the truck to pull off with a final "I'll burn your fucking nigger house down" and then walk back across the street to pick up the trash I had just been bombarded with.

In the passenger seat of the truck every day was Keith's sister Kristen. A sixth-grader with perfect freckles, offset by deep brown eyes. She would look down, allowing me some dignity by pretending it wasn't happening. At school she would smile a soft apology in the halls. I would daydream of ripping her brother out of his truck and then kissing her on the lips. I wanted to touch her milk white skin. But each day would end with her glumly studying her shoes while her big brother spat on me.

I started hiding out in the school bathroom so I would miss my bus home. After the last yellow coach would pull off I would sneak out past the janitors and walk the two miles to my house. That worked for about a week until Keith got wise to my strategy and waited, driving slowly next to me spitting and screaming the entire way.

I figured my only choice now was not to go to school at all. I was sick with a fever for days after I learned to hold the thermometer near my bedside lamp to raise the mercury. Eating an entire package of Ex-Lax chocolate kept me out of school for half a week. One early spring afternoon I plucked poison ivy out by its roots and rubbed it all over my face, chest and back. That night as my body caught fire and the rash spread from my hairline to my waistband I was positive I had bought myself a solid week's vacation. I was wrong. My mother shook me awake the next morning holding a big tube of salve. By the time I got to school I looked like a voodoo priest covered head to toe in the white paste of calamine lotion.

Eventually the sicknesses became real. I woke up in the middle of the night, doubled over in pain, screaming. My mother came running and within minutes had me packed into the station wagon on our way to the hospital. The doctors gave me a chalky liquid to drink and a loud clacking machine took X-rays of my stomach. They spoke quietly to my mother about things as benign as an ulcer and as serious as stomach cancer. They decided to keep me for further observation.

That week in the hospital was an oasis. I was fed a steady diet of red Jell-O and the nurses called me "Nate the great," running their soft, clean fingers through my hair. I never wanted to leave.

After the tests came back inconclusive I was discharged. The doctors simply said I had a "nervous stomach" and asked my mom if I was under any stress. My mother said "Of course not, he's only eight years old."

The nurses threw me a going away party and gave me a red Corvette Matchbox car with its silver engine sticking out through the hood. They couldn't understand why I wasn't happier to be going home.

The principal had called my mother and was concerned that it was only May and I had already missed twenty-four days of school. She promised him I would be there Monday.

Sunday night I was curled up on the couch while my dad sat in his chair with his scotch and water watching CBS's *60 Minutes*. Dozing off, I was startled awake by a familiar sound. Footsteps marching, voices full of rage screaming in unison. I opened my eyes to see white robes carrying placards declaring "death to race mixing" and "white is right." The footage was of a Klan rally in Chicago and my stomach instantly twisted into knots. But then the TV showed something amazing. Unlike the passive faces of Torrington, in Chicago people black, brown, and white lined the sidewalk pelting the now fleeing Klansmen with rocks and bottles. Riot police moved in to protect the Klan and the crowd started fighting with the officers. The camera fixed in on one white man with a bandanna covering the lower half of his face, his eyes watery and bloodshot from tear gas, repeatedly kicking a fallen Klansmen on the ground.

My father shook his head in disgust saying that was no way to solve the problem, but I was transfixed. That seemed to me to be a very effective way. If there had been even one person to stand up for me, to take to Keith Kelly's pickup with a crowbar you better believe he wouldn't have been there the next day. As far as I was concerned that was the definition of a problem solved.

I felt energized the next morning. I had been gone from school for over a week and looked forward to seeing my friends. Even class wasn't so bad; Mrs. Pierson decided since I had just come out of the hospital I could skip the math quiz and read quietly to catch up on English.

At the end of the day I stood wrestling and laughing with my friend Brian in the line for our bus. We got on and took our normal seats in the back. As we pulled away from school my stomach tightened as the rusted blue pickup fell in behind us. I looked out the back window and Keith Kelly's pockmarked face smiled back at me.

The bus stopped at Candlebirch farm and Mrs. Finch the driver pulled back the big lever opening the door for me. I said goodbye to Brian and slowly walked off. As the bus pulled away and the truck drove up I caught a spray of phlegm on my cheek. "You fucking nigger, hope your whole Jew family dies!"

Torrington, Connecticut, was a far way from Chicago, and there was no one to throw rocks or bottles. Just a fat white pig, waiting.

**AARON BEDARD**

Bane

## *One Summer Knight*

There they went again.

Neighborhood maniacs going buck wild, throwing fists and feet from every angle. At first it seemed to be a three-on-one situation, which was ugly enough, but soon a second wave of friends rushed into the frame, sucking all the challenge and drama from the scene, as it went from being a street fight to a brutal beating. It was hard to imagine what the poor guy must have done to bring such chaos into his world, but it only took seconds for him to stop trying to stand up for himself and, through obvious experience, fold into a ball on the sidewalk while an avalanche of sneakers and boots rained down upon him.

Nick literally had a front-row seat for the whole mess, in a window booth of a restaurant, where he sat alone, trying to enjoy a salad. He could see every blow, could see into their eyes. Some were actually shining, enjoying every frantic second, while others looked so focused and furious that he started to worry that they may not stop until this guy was dead.

People out on the busy street, which the locals referred to as the Avenue, were starting to turn their attention to the ruckus, stopping in their tracks, watching from the doors and windows of storefronts. Though no one seemed to be *doing* anything.

Even when someone inside the restaurant cried out, "Jesus, someone call the cops!" nothing really happened.

The Veg Edge was a small, quiet health food restaurant, only a few blocks from Nick's apartment. He found himself there several times a week. He didn't usually like the lone booth by the window, however; all of the activity out on the strip was generally too distracting, even when the locals weren't beating the daylights out of each other right in broad daylight. He preferred the quiet booths in the back where he could spread his textbooks out and get some work done. But there was no homework due tonight, he had actually finished his second semester of medical school that very day and had come to the Veg Edge to unwind over a light meal and a Batman graphic novel. But instead, he was forced to sit and note the difference between a fight in a comic book and a fight out in the streets.

An old woman in an apron burst out from the pizza place next door, screaming and waving a finger at the blur of oversized, white T-shirts, baggy denim, and silver chains. This didn't stop them from stomping their victim into the pavement. No one missed a blow. One of the boys simply turned and swore defiantly back into her face, sending her storming right back through the door from which she came.

Nick looked down at Batman, dancing across the pages of his comic book, kicking ass, saving the day. He longed for that type of fearlessness and resolution, to be able to just dive headfirst into messes like this one. To put a stop to what was begging to be stopped . . . as long as he could remember there had been that pull to do something heroic, to be the one to save the earth from a meteor. But instead he had grown into a tall, awkward, medical student. Who, at twenty-two, still found inspiration, as well as his idea of right and wrong, good and evil, inside the pages of the comic books he never managed to outgrow.

It wasn't the first time he'd been forced to watch some minor injustice unfold, filled with fear and hesitation, knowing exactly what needed to be done but being frozen solid, faced with the most disappointing part of himself.

The Avenue wasn't even in a bad neighborhood, not an easy claim in the city of Baltimore, where the ghettos stretched to every corner of the city limits and beyond. Where any street you found yourself on seemed to lead, eventually, to an area where you would rather not be. But outside Nick's window was supposedly one of the city's safer places. Tucked away between a sprawling park and Johns Hopkins University, it was home to a delicate mix of college kids, local hipsters, and the white working-class types who had lived among its row houses for generations. It was the kind of place you were supposed to be able to walk around at night. People grew gardens in their yards, kids and dogs played freely, safe from stray bullets and used needles. The Avenue was its centerpiece, the main drag, where restaurants and boutiques stood side by side with dive bars, convenience stores, and pawnshops. Though every once in a while things did get crazy out there and it was almost always at the hands of young men with bad tattoos and huge T-shirts.

On the sidewalk the fight was over. The victim lay in a heap. One of his attackers reached down and grabbed him by the hair, forcing him to look skyward. He barked a few last words right into his swollen face and then spit directly into it, before letting the poor bastard drop back down to the pavement.

Satisfied, the gang turned and walked away, laughing and tapping knuckles.

The kid rolled onto his back, brought his palms to his eyes as if just waking. There was nothing Nick could see to separate him from his attackers. He looked like every other young man born and bred in that corner of the city. Sometimes it was hard to tell if they were actually teenagers who looked as hard and weathered as the thirty-year-olds or if they were thirty-year-olds who still dressed like teenagers.

Slowly he made his way to his feet, wiping his face with the sleeve of his sweatshirt and spitting mouthfuls of black onto the sidewalk. He didn't seem all that devastated or shaken by what he'd just been through, even waving off the help of a passerby, as if it had all just been a normal part of his day.

Nick watched as he walked out of view and was then forced to sit and ponder, not for the first time, the one ingredient that could make life in an otherwise decent little neighborhood so trying. Those roaming packs of bored teenagers, clogging storefronts and street corners, the threat of violence, forever simmering, just beneath their surface. Nick had been living among them in a tiny basement apartment since he was a sophomore and, in the three years since, had witnessed his share of savage behavior.

One night on the Avenue, he passed a boy being loaded into an ambulance. He'd been stabbed in the stomach with a screwdriver. His girlfriend was crying on the curb, screaming to the police that he hadn't done anything. Another night he came out of a convenience store just as a gang of them was walking by. One of them, carrying a large, Styrofoam cup, stopped, turned, and then spit a mouthful of whatever was in the cup right into the face of a man who was merely standing on the corner, talking on his cell phone. Completely shocked, the man stood helpless, cell phone by his side, face dripping, and watched as the gang continued down the street, as if nothing out of the ordinary had occurred. There was the morning he woke up to find the passenger side windows of his and every other car on the block smashed to pieces. Nothing had been stolen and everyone knew who did it, it was simply *them*, vast and vague enough for no one to do anything about it.

Or the eeriest night of all: while driving home late from the school library, the Avenue was quiet and deserted, except for four shadowy figures sitting against the front entrance of a liquor store, blasting a boom box. Nick had to do a double take to believe his eyes. There were no faces. All four of them appeared to be wearing gas masks.

Some nights he would lie awake. He could feel them out there, running around unchecked, un-judged. On the other side of his room sat a white cardboard box filled with the adventures of Daredevil, Captain America, and Green Lantern, of men who were ready, at the drop of a hat, to do whatever it took to set things right.

Why not him?

Because he hadn't hurt anyone in his life, because he came from upper-crust parents in a peaceful Massachusetts suburb. A scary night where Nick came from was when the police made you pour out your beer and sent you home. People hurt you by gossiping behind your back, by not inviting you to their parties. Nobody was out in the streets fighting for their lives.

But, God, did anything and everything feel possible to him

at that moment, sitting there, picking at a salad that his stomach was too knotted to accept. It was a strange time for Nick, he'd been feeling off for months, restless, right on the ledge, looking down.

Very suddenly, every second that ticked by seemed to hold in its grasp the lure and the promise that he could be more than just some quiet, overachieving medical student. Somewhere deep within him a dark-hearted beast was slowly stirring awake.

When he had sat to eat that evening he had no idea what to do with his summer, he had three wide-open months stretched out before him, the longest block of completely free time he'd had in forever. No summer courses, no tutoring job, no track practice, and no girlfriend. It had been nearly a year since Kathryn had broken up with him, although sometimes it still hurt like it was only a week ago. No one was waiting for him, nothing was expected of him and for the past week he'd been haunted by the feeling that this may the very last time his slate would ever be this clean, and he had no idea what to do with it.

"Take a drive cross-country," Dr. Beacon, his anatomy professor, had suggested a few days earlier, when Nick stayed late to help clean up after a lab. "Every young man should see this country through a bug-stained windshield."

"Yeah, maybe," Nick replied. "I just feel like there's gotta be some kinda excitement for me out there. I know that the next four years of school are gonna go by just as fast as the first four, and before I know it I'm gonna turn around and be this thirty-year-old guy who never really had any idea how crazy or . . . or epic, life can be."

"That's hogwash," Beacon waved. "It's never too late to stir the pot up a bit. A few years ago when the missus and I were feeling restless and uninspired, you know what we did? We took a skydiving course! Now you wanna talk about shaking up the regularness of life, try looking at the world from thirty thousand feet."

Still, Nick couldn't help but think there had to be an even more dynamic way to lay to rest a youth that, to this point, had almost entirely consisted of preparing to be a man, a doctor, just like his father.

Anything would be better than sitting around his humid apartment, reading comic books and making obsessive trips to his computer to check for e-mails from her. Signing onto instant messenger to see if she was also logged on. Too stubborn or wounded to start a conversation, he would simply stare at her name on his buddy list, Koalakid84, and wonder how she could really not have anything left to say to him. Tortured by the thoughts of who she must be talking to instead.

Maybe it was time to deal with himself, with the city he called home, with the neighborhood that confused him and all of the little troublemakers who kept him up at night. No more running off to sunny Santa Barbara the moment he had a few free days from school, like he'd been doing since the weekend when he and Kathryn went from living three minutes from each other to over three thousand miles.

She had been weaving her vines around his heart since they rode the bus together to grade school. They played in the same soccer league, rode their bikes together to the library on weekends, wrote letters to each other from their respective summer camps, and stood side by side through the death of pets and grandparents. At twelve they shared their first kiss, exchanged plastic engagement rings at thirteen, and by high school you couldn't say one of their names without the other.

So, when they found themselves heading off to opposite coasts for college there really wasn't even a question of, "how will we make this work?" Nick simply guaranteed that they would. Whatever it was going to take to get them through the years apart he would do.

For the first year it felt like he was on a plane or in her dorm room more than he was in his own. They met back up in Massachusetts for all of the major holidays and once he got his own place she even made a few visits to Baltimore. The plan had always been that when she graduated from Antioch she would come to stay with him in Baltimore while he finished his MD.

Even when they couldn't be together he fought to give her all the attention his day would allow with e-mails and three-hour-long IM conversations. For the first two years, every day they weren't together, they called each other to say goodnight. Throughout the day his cell phone was constantly vibrating in his pocket with text messages.

*Hey cutie I just touched a starfish!!*

*Can you believe they don't have Count Chocula in this grocery store?*

*Holy mother of Christ this professor will put u to sleep . . . just wanna be back on yr dad's big comfy wraparound watching a movie . . . not watching a movie xox*

Even when she decided, last year, that she would stay in California beyond graduation, take some courses at UCLA, it didn't occur to Nick that she could be slipping through his fingers. It wasn't until his final visit, last August, that it became clear things had changed. They hadn't seen each other since the Fourth of July, yet the entire week was strained. She seemed distracted, cold, and short with him far more than usual. She kept mentioning friends he had never heard of before, *Tom said this, Danny and Alex did that*. Her face constantly buried in that cell phone of hers, sending and receiving text messages that made her grin far more than he was able to make her. The day before he had to leave he sat her down to ask what was going on. She told him she was stressed over the upcoming semester and had friends out there who were going through the same thing. That night he fell asleep on her couch while she talked on the phone in her room. She never came out to get him.

At the airport the next morning, he looked and could see that she had really bloomed. His smiling, high school sweetheart from all the pictures in all the scrapbooks was no more. The way she talked was different, her clothes were smaller, more stylish. That once quiet, understated beauty had given way to something staggering. The California sun had gently tanned her face, sent streaks of gold through her hair. Her green eyes had never shined so electric.

A week later she ended it in an e-mail. Claimed that the distance had become too great for her to bear. That she wasn't ready to be some doctor's wife. That he would find somebody better. In the month that followed, the miles between them grew wider than any map could show. His every instinct screamed for him to fight harder, to fly to Santa Barbara and fall to his knees, but somehow he knew in his head and what remained of his heart that it would do no good.

He tried to stay in touch but his messages fell flat. Tear-streaked voice mails went unanswered for days, weeks. While he was home at Christmas, she stopped by to drop off a wine basket for his parents and a leather wallet for him. Standing there, forcing awkward conversation, he realized it had been three months since he'd heard her voice at all.

There would be no lying on a Santa Barbara beach this summer, smiling about what their house would be like, what color the kid's room would be.

The girl he loved was gone.

With nothing left to do and no shoulder to cry on, he threw himself into his school work; impressed every professor he came across, found himself published in one of the more prestigious medical journals, was offered the residency of his choice, and little by little his knuckles healed. But in the end he knew he was just going through the motions, doing well because he didn't know how not to do well. None of it meant anything without her. His every road, no matter how well paved or brightly lit, seemed to lead right to the same dead end.

Back out on the Avenue the shadows were growing longer, the sun sinking below the tree line. Nick hadn't taken a bite of food in over an hour. He was a hawk perched on a wire, watching the after-work race of humans darting in and out of banks, restaurants, and liquor stores, everyone in a rush to get somewhere, anywhere but where they were. Among them a large crew of teenagers was ambling its way down the other side of the street, led by two menacing pit bulls on thick chain leashes. The gang stopped to talk with a couple of trashy, teenage girls pushing a baby stroller. Nick recognized one of the boys from the fight earlier; he had been right there in the mix, stomping his Timberlands down mercilessly.

Now he was just standing right out in the open, like he was untouchable, cigar sticking out of the side of his cocked baseball hat, laughing openly, as if he had already forgotten about the whole ordeal. Nick didn't know where the crew would go that night or what kind of trouble they would cause, but the thought of them being able to go home afterward and sleep with big, safe, smiles on their faces, began to tear him apart inside. Nobody was watching them and they knew it. There was no balance of power and, in a flash, it suddenly became ferociously clear exactly what Nick needed to do with his summer.

What he needed to be.

Could he do it? Did it even make sense? Would he really wear some kind of costume . . . carry a gun? Creep around in the shadows waiting for something to happen . . . begging for something to happen? What would he call himself? The Fear? Chief Justice? The Crusader?

Was he crazy?

Or had his whole life been leading to that night, sitting there staring out a restaurant window, all of the puzzle pieces clicking together.

He could pull it off; he'd excelled at everything he'd ever set his mind to.

Well everything but one. There would always be the one wild card that was Kathryn, forever blemishing a mantel, back in Massachusetts, that was bursting with trophies, medals, and accolades. If his father had instilled anything in him it was that whatever was worth doing was worth doing right. And if he were going to do this thing, it would be with the same focus and intensity that he brought to all of his endeavors. If he couldn't be stronger he would be smarter, if not faster then he would be more frightening than anything they had ever known.

Whatever he could possibly need was right there on the Internet, a virtual Batcave, sitting on the desk in his bedroom, filled with weapons, gadgets, and crime reports, 1,001 ways to kill a man, just a click away.

It wouldn't be like it was in the comic books and he knew it. He wasn't one of those strange guys up at the comic shop on weekends, discussing the physics of Wolverine's claws. There would be no bursting through the window in the nick of time, no clever remarks in speech bubbles but, then again, these weren't exactly super villains he was dealing with. They were some of the softest Baltimore had to offer, bored bullies and petty dealers, upset because they didn't live in the hell that existed on the other side of town, or in their beloved rap videos, so they tried, with all their might, to create one for themselves.

There was no rationalizing with kids like that, threats won't do and you can't throw a sixteen-year-old in jail. There was only one way to get through to them.

It was all spelled out, right there in bloodstains on the sidewalk.

You needed to stomp the evil from their very souls, had to keep them in a constant state of panic.

It would mean yanking some young punk into an alley, placing a pistol right to his forehead.

*"This is just a warning."*

Close enough to smell the stale cigarettes on his breath.

*"You tell your boys that I am watching."*

Tiny marble beads forming on a bottom lip.

*"These streets do not belong to you."*

All of that tough guy bravado being sucked right from him, like a balloon, as he stands face-to-face with the masked avenger.

*"The next time you see me you will not hear a word . . . do you understand?"*

Eyes filled with that crystal-clear realization of being nowhere near ready to die, he slowly nods his head.

Then, once he was done with them and the streets were safe at last, he could move on to worse neighborhoods, to the projects on the other side of the park, to the places even the police didn't want to go.

His heart was racing full speed now, a fire raging in his belly, melting the doubt.

The two girls and the gang went their separate ways, one of the girls flipping them off over her shoulder, the boys laughing and disappearing into the night.

The time was now, not later, not soon, but right now.

They were out there, searching for the next night to ruin. The whole city was holding its breath, waiting for him. No super-powers necessary. It was as simple as marching right down to the pawnshop before it closed. If they wouldn't sell him a pistol, they would sell him a stun gun, if not a stun gun, then mace. He needed nothing more than a hoodie, a ski mask, and the will to do the unthinkable, not because he wanted to, but because no one else would.

His every nerve ending was alive and screaming as he rose, grabbed his things, and moved quickly to the register. A voice deep inside, begging his mind to stop spinning and be reason-able, to think it through for just one more minute.

---

He could see the ambulance sirens, police cruisers blocking off the street. His father's disappointment as he quietly shook his head.

His poor mother's shrieking voice.

"He did what?! To who?!?! I knew it! Knew those goddamn Superman books were gonna lead to no good."

Medical school, the future he had worked so hard for, spinning down the drain.

In line at the register, the music was too loud, his mouth bone dry. He could feel his pulse as clearly as if there were a blood pressure strap around his arm. There was no turning back. Get down to the pawnshop, see what they'll sell him. Soon it would be late, the bars would close and the streets would grow quiet. The ones not out looking for trouble would be home in bed and those that were would be easy to find, out there in the alleys with the rats, on the corners with the serpents. It was like he could already feel the brass knuckles, cold and heavy in his hand. He would find the biggest one, the worst of the bunch, grab that motherfucker right by the throat and . . .

"Was everything all right?" It was his waitress, pulling him off the roller coaster in his mind

"Um, yeah . . . yes, fine thanks."

"Sorry about that ruckus out there earlier." She shook her head. "So stupid."

"It's not your fault. I'm sorry I hogged up that booth for so long."

"Oh, no worries," she said. "If it wasn't you it'd just be some art dork reading *The Bell Jar* or something."

"Not sure I'm much better." He smiled, holding up his Batman book.

"Oh, I'd say you're a hell of a lot better."

"Really? You into comics?"

"A little bit."

From under the front counter she presented a small black handbag with a lone, metal pin attached. It was The Punisher logo.

"Wow, very cool. Yeah, I love The Punisher stuff."

"Guy'll fuck you up for real." She smiled. "You go to Hopkins?"

"Yeah. You?" Nick realized that this was going past the point of friendly register banter. Her smile seemed genuine, nervous.

"No, MICA." She rolled her eyes, referring to the city's art institute and pointed both thumbs inward. "Art dork."

Nick chuckled as she leaned back against the counter behind her, brought her shoulders up high, and sighed.

"So, I told myself if you came in here today that . . . that I would tell you about what's going on at The Charles tonight."

He didn't know what to make of all this but suddenly his ears weren't ringing and his skin wasn't so sticky inside his dress shirt, the universe slowing down again.

The girls who worked at the Veg Edge didn't seem like the types who would have any interest in a guy like him. They dyed their hair and wore cool clothes, listened to bands he'd never heard of, hung out in clubs he'd never been to. But there she was, smiling right at him in a yellow track jacket. On her hips he could see matching tattoos, disappearing down into her beat-up jeans. Thick, dark hair piled atop her head in a rush of a ponytail. She was the kind of girl that Kathryn would have dismissed as a freak, but leaning there against that counter, chewing on the corner of her lip, she seemed to be about the most interesting thing Nick had seen in forever.

"Why, what's going on at The Charles?" he asked. The urgency of the sun falling and the pawnshop closing growing duller by the second, softening its grip. It felt like someone was lifting a concrete slab from his chest.

"Well, you know they have midnight movies on some Fridays, right?"

"No, actually I'm pretty clueless when it comes to what's going on around here." The Charles was the city's independent movie theater, and in all his years in town, Nick had not been there once.

"Oh, man, the midnight movies are great and tonight they're having two!"

"Yeah? What are they showing?"

"They are showing," she paused dramatically, "*Kill Bill* parts one AND two. I mean, c'mon, you gotta love those movies, right?"

"Yeah, totally. I think Tarantino's great and, actually, I've only seen the first part, so . . . Midnight tonight, huh, and you're . . . you're going?"

"Sure am, me and a big bucket of popcorn."

It was a strange sensation, smiling and not being able to stop. He could feel it stretching across a face that hadn't felt so out of control in months.

"And c'mon, if you think about it, you really kind of need to see the second part."

"It's true," he said. "And oddly enough my schedule just so happens to be wide open between twelve and four tonight."

She laughed hard, it was a great laugh and already Nick couldn't wait to hear it again.

"Yeah, that sounds really fun," he added. "I'd . . . I'd like to go see those tonight."

"OK, great." She smiled, swinging an invisible sword into an invisible foe. "Wanna meet in the lobby around a quarter 'til?"

"Sounds good, I'll be there," he said. "What's your name anyway? I'm Nick."

"I'm Tanner," she replied as a party of five came through the front door.

"All right, well, I'll let you get back to work and, um . . . I'll definitely see you down there at a quarter of."

"Very cool, I'll see you later, Nick," she said and came around the counter to seat the customers.

Out in the street the cool summer air flung its arms around his neck. He forgot about the pawnshop all together and turned left to head home. As he passed by a pair of Eminem look-alikes, propped up on the back of a bus stop bench, he defied his every instinct and chose to look right into their bored and soulless eyes.

"Evening boys," he offered, brightly.

The first kid, maybe fifteen, cocked his head in disbelief.

"The fuck you say to me, faggot," he sneered, with a sickening accent.

"Come on back here and I'll whoop yo' muthafuckin' ass," the other shouted at Nick's back.

He would deal with them some other time. Tonight he had a grin that would not fade as he floated on down the Avenue, into the endless possibilities, beneath a thousand blinking stars.

**RYAN HUNTER**
**Envy on the Coast**

## *Auditions with Our Heavenly Father*

*Dear Mother,*
*I heard the news . . . Father told me it was true.*

*Stage 1..........................................................3,343 Questions*

*What retribution do you owe? Purity, honesty, and charity*
*fashion your bones. This cancerous but temporary plague is*
*lacking a simple sense of reason. I picture you, before the altar,*
*face towards the crucifix screaming "treason."*

*Stage 2.......................................................................Theory*

*Prayer gives way to postulation and it seems clear . . . you*
*are a candidate; the meager explanation, in which the cancer*
*sought to permeate. Though there shall be tests, trials, and*
*tribulations, your mercy requites with viscous patience.*

*Stage 3.....................................Understanding hallucination*

*Now I'm lost in your eyes, as you're engulfed in a sea of*
*white linens in a hospital bed; a young, angelic presence*
*steadily hovers above your bed. She is the heavenly scout,*

*surveying your incessant compassion, just observing that your heart still has portions left to ration.*

*Stage 4...........................................................The procedure*

*Now I hold your tears as a ransom . . . within the palm of my hand. Your trepidation loses vigor as you begin to understand. We live in wicked, mundane waiting rooms, but the destinations barely compare; though you comprehend the purpose, I catch you basking in despair. Not to worry; for I shall stand beside you always. Mother, I'll stand beside you always. Blessed are you . . . the very first to ever care.*

*Stage 5.....................................................................Her smile*

*Broadcasted from a hospital bed . . . this was only a test. This was only a test.*

*Love,*
*Your Son*

## SAL BOSSIO
Envy on the Coast

*My heart is pounding the whole way there.*

I arrive in disbelief and can only stare at those buried eyes as
you scream, "it's not fair!"
As I walk further in, you come running towards the stairs.
Our shoulders touch, I reach across my fingers through your hair.
Everyone is scattered all dressed in black.
His sister starts to shout, "I want him back, I want him back!"
Your eyelids shut, you place your head upon me in distress.
Adrienne, I just can't stand to see you like this.
Allow my collar be the place where you let your tears rest.
Please don't worry girl; you know god only takes the best.
Goodbye, Goodbye. I owe you this much, I'll be your medication
Goodbye, Goodbye. I own you this much; I'm a safe addiction.

## PETER WENTZ
**Fall Out Boy**

Tonight we lie in a city that doesn't belong to either of us. From
the penthouse it looks like a movie set. The grays are too perfect.
It feels lit for a camera. The moon is too yellow and perfect.
Babygirl, with pupils the size of baby worlds.
She said, "I just want you to know that I never do things like
this."
But only people who always 'do things like this' say lines like
that.
I reply, "There are cobwebs on the zippers of all my jeans."
And I'm thinking God must be a hack for writing such shitty
dialogue like that.
And I'm thinking it's lines like that which set you free. They are
your alibi.
They are your 'get out of jail free' card.
We are clumsy as we make our moves.
Moonlight makes for fools.
The best offense is a good defense, or is it the other way
around? Either way, we're both checking the scoreboard in a
hazy kind of way.
I'd invade a country for the small of your back.
Fingertip lover.
When we were young we spent our nights sleeping on
hardwood floors,
spitting on lottery tickets, and throwing away collectors items.

We didn't have to dodge flashes or try to sleep through worry. It's funny the things that cross your mind as she fumbles with your belt.

"Why do you write like sex and love are the only things that make your heart beat?"

I work her buckle.

"Because you've got it all backwards, they are the only things that make my heart stop."

Her blond hair hangs on her eyes. The headlines would call her a bombshell.

But it hangs like a black cloud over my head when I lie under her. I almost slip and tell her.

"And friends, sex, love, regret, and revenge are all in the perfect proportions. They've always got my head swimming. It's gonna end the world."

Had a fling with second chances, but it wasn't my thing. Spent the last ten years throwing up, lovesick in sinks.

To the gutters were always heaving, out the doors were always leaving.

My mind quickly turns to excuses and alibis. How could you be upset, I am on a mirror for a ruined culture, but I settle on kissing her forehead. Sometimes you gotta play it safe.

"Potions for foxes" is whispering in our ears. Stuff a towel under the door to keep out the rumors. I'm supposed to be somewhere else with someone else, so is she.

Your petals bloom on my skin and something changes in me. I want to be better and different—to have my body belong to you, not memories and the dirt of this ruined planet.

"When I'm deep over my head, there doesn't feel like there is much of a difference between fucking and a fistfight."

A one-night standoff.

Kind of safe inside the green zone of a love affair.

But the stagecoach always turns back into a pumpkin in the light of day.

No one gives a fuck about eyes that keep leaking.

Always hushing the headboard on beds that keep creaking.

"If I wasn't writing words and singing into microphones, I'm pretty sure I would make a good divorce lawyer or mercy killer."

I tell her I have to get up at 6 to go back to work.

"But this is my work. Trashing people's emotions. Cataloging our dreams and hopes. Putting our faith in a can, sealing it for freshness, and selling it off. I turn a profit every single time."

My alarm goes off at 5:30. But we are both still awake.

She has a plane. I have words.

"I am an examiner. I am an outsider. I am inside the clock trying to figure out how all of the pulleys and levers work."

"I am the feeling in Dorothy's house right before the tornado picked it up and dropped in on the Witch. I am the buzzing and humming.

The dog barking. The lady screaming."

We get in cars with the windows tinted jet black. At the corner she turns left and I turn right.

My head moves too fast. Don't bother, try and keep up.

I turn right again. And then again, back in front of my hotel I walk up the stairs and into my room. I am asleep by 6:00 AM.

It's summertime 15 floors up.

Heat waves don't got shit on me.

I sweat this one out. Asleep. With the phone off the hook.

The truth will do that to you.

"I'd love to take all the best storytellers, the greatest lovers and liars and lock them underground. Suffocate them all."

I love you in a holding your hair back kind of way.

I'm up to my hips in dreams, crying crocodile tears into a swamp in this town.

And you, you couldn't like me but I think you could love me.

"Then with them all blue and dead, I would be the best."

## CHINA SOUL
`Minor Celebration`

### Dramatic Monologue

Call it.

"I don't know what that's supposed to mean," I told him
and clicked the light switch off and then on again
and he tap, tap, tapped on the empty glass
that stood on the empty table.
I said "maybe I'll just leave and get on a boat or something."
He told me "don't be stupid, you hate the ocean."
I asked him how he knew and that maybe I had changed my
mind
He said he just did.

He just did.

That's when he looked at me and I looked at him
and I told him one ear looked higher than the other;
that I had never noticed before.
He said it was because half his head was down in the ground
and the other was somewhere else
I asked him where and he said he didn't quite know
that maybe it was back there

way back there.

Maybe he left it on some coatrack that
slouched down, sick from its own antiquity
in that gentlemen's lounge he used to go to
when he was feeling lonely
I asked him what lonely was and he shook his head
he said it's when you can't think of anything else to call yourself
I told him that I could think of lots of things to call him
he shook his again

just like that.

And everything was falling
I closed my eyes and counted to ten in my head
I saw the sea and its waves and decided it wasn't so bad
the next time we met he was looking up at the sky
and recited to me each animal he saw in the clouds
I said I couldn't see them and he seemed mad
when I got up to leave he asked me why
because, I said, I love the sea.

## MATTHEW ROSKOWSKI
Delilah in the Calm

### *Roll Up My Sympathy*

There's a spindle in the middle of the town rolling up the scenery. It spins and spins until it's just the concrete and me. In the morning it unfolds like a tapestry through the parks and the city streets. And there we stand, just like we've always been. It's you and me until the bitter end.

## MATTHEW CLEGG

Caitlin Going and the All the Way's

## *Which Way?*

The Sky pierces them, only the sky. Orange, gray, purple, red; none could force its way through. The tall one old, the small one new. Wailing sound, dust and will power, tracing the screen with the blue light tool. The case fell to the bed. Late. He wasn't accustomed to his own hands. It's just one of those days, the snow glides down. How will I charge through the walls, the shores, the cellophane around the fruit? Is there redemption in citrus?

**MARK ROSE**

Spitalfield

*Vocals/Guitar*

May I step out of character?
Or is it unlike me to do that?
Tell me.
Sometimes I forget what I am like in real life.

## STEVEN LEFEBVRE
Sophia

### feeding bob potter

Dreamer, Dreamer
Do you know what's in store?

I hold back

Long walk back through poverty and hatred
In my golden sandals, what a long walk back it was

Murder, was it me who held the gun?
Sinners, and we didn't even know it

I don't lie, don't cheat, don't draw your blood

The Church is bricked in gold and the children are so hungry
My hands, my hands my greedy hands
The eye is getting smaller, the needle has stopped threading
My hands, my hands my greedy hands

I don't want my heart to want this way
I will follow you
Through the eye of the needle

**CHI CHENG**

Deftones

## *The Death of a Family Guilt*

Exhibit a     she was sexually molested by her stepfather
for years—and when she finally came
clean—about it—her mother made her testify
to a court—that she lied
so they could continue to be a
family—at least for another couple
years—

Exhibit b     He was pistol-whipped in front of
his brothers and sisters by his father
and when his mother couldn't get the old man
to lay off and asked him
why—
he said it was because the boy
had his eyes

Exhibit c     she hadn't spoken to her father in years
because when she was young
her and her father's best friend
were having relations—and when she
told him about it—he called her
A liar and wrote her

off—continuing on with his pal
to this day

Exhibit d        he contracted HIV in the early '90s from being
monogamous
to his girlfriend—who had been raped
while they were dating

Exhibit a        she tried to overdose on pills
in front of their son—telling him
that she was going to be with
god—and would watch over him
before she lay down
beside him—on the living room
floor

Exhibit b        he got to take the day off
school—when he was 13—because
his father had shot his dog
and he woke up with her
in a Glad trash bag—and needing
to be buried

Exhibit c        she was raped and beaten
by an ex-boyfriend—who used
to give her panties to other women
he was fucking—then
shit on her clothes—when she
tried—to
        leave—

Exhibit d      he used to have to massage his father's
back and feet—after
being—beaten

Exhibit e      her husband used to beat her so
soundly—the children would watch
her—mop up
her own blood
when he was done
     And
on Monday—Feb 9
my younger brother
got a thin yellow rope
and hung himself
  in the garage
so—
  while we all got
our stories to
  tell
his are up
for grabs—or
misinterpretation
and I'm sure
at some point
I'll fuck one up
and he won't be there
    to correct—
      ME

## Murder, Prostitution and Other Forms of Democracy and the Institution of Marriage

He had married—his secret mother
wanting—to be a whore
they fucked—like they were trying
to extract the ingredients of
the horizon, from
each other—and she could
swallow—the ocean
at the mouth—as he tried to push
the tides—for her—and
in the time it takes
for an ocean liner
to sink—they had only reached
a fetal shore puberty—still
madly in love
years later—he would quietly
count her—freckles when she slept
　　so
when people ask
　　him
why don't you write
　　about
politics—or
the fucking
　　war

He could reply
  I do—
you just ain't hearing
  it
    Right

## BRANDON WRONSKI

Dead Letter Diaries

### *Progress in Part*

Morning sunlight always does find her way;
Whether sleep does find or sleep escape
'Twill find a way to make me weak today;
If knowledge is key why reiterate?
In this new light I think I'll find a cure
For those who love and live to be deceived,
For times when abolition was sure
That all its strife could be for once relieved,
That its worries could be sent out to sea;
Progress in part becomes winning the heart;
Is everyone I know the same indeed?
In no way did I believe in this remark;
Flowers did bloom, untouched by man for whom
Did first attempt to inhabit the moon?

## Sand in Context

Take this sand out of context. Let's use it to make substances
transparent to the eyes. Make it look like fields after rain. Let
this "glass" reflect the beauty of the flowers on the right. And
let it soak up every ounce of color that disrupts it on the left.
Let our invention become obsolete and cut a trail to new
technology. We want green fields, so when it's snowing vibrant
white let's replace it with the color on the right. As sand
becomes glass, the glass becomes an information center on a
disk. Which in turn becomes our trust or should we hold it in
our hands. One time I'd like to see this for what it is. Should we
hold on to technology that will slip away like the sand?

## *Kodiak*

Kodiak aside to the sea a wife skinks

Edit one skid

Lies, power the airflows immense; oak trees wiped now

Sell Vesuvius

SAD

Solid

Each day

Foil

Lording kerns

Joker this Pompeii

Lockers

Joker this tsunami 9.0

Gilding

Boulder 7, 4

Lore the rest through your mountain fall

\Kite

Just every that kiss lady low

Hushed sea and the sky splits

Shays soils sized

Due dim doodled decked

\Key

D duh

She put the Kodak aside to see me in modern light because I can't escape the rain
And I said to her what do you mean? What skies will fall and seas will spit out steam?

## ADAM PANIC
Adam Panic

### Hello me.

As the prelude to a show
(Proving that heirs leave space)
You'll find yourself in a bond between what is right and what
you've gone to.
I'll hurry to place the papers in a fireproof safe,
only to find it drenched with gas and marked with postage to
be sent into space.
I turned my head to the left.
Hello me.
I put a promise charm on the dresser and backed away after that.
The note said that I'm leaving and I'm going to the front door.
You can meet me there if you want.
I turned my head to the left again.
Hello me.
Now this is the plan:
I'm getting out of this sand that's lengthening my reach for air.
The sound of the grains crushing themselves is deafening.
Each one is saying hello to me.
They're punching holes in my ears.
They're making me sweat.
So I'll give up my space to you,
but please leave attempts for me.

**JOHN NOLAN**
Straylight Run

## *I Might Be Wrong*

It's nine o'clock in the morning at Los Angeles International Airport, but to me it feels like seven o'clock last night. Or it might be six o'clock later this evening. Or eight o'clock tomorrow night. For the past two weeks I've been on the opposite side of the world, where the time is roughly thirteen hours different from the time it is in the part of the world where I live. I've been on a plane for the past fourteen hours and now I've got a two-hour layover in Los Angeles, where the time is three hours earlier than it is in my home in New York. So I'm pretty unsure of time at the moment.

My friend Shaun and I are searching for some sort of restaurant/bar to sit down in and wait out our last hours before the final flight home. We spot a little place right near our gate and walk in to sit down. I think that I might be hungry but I don't really know. My body is as unsure of the time as my mind. Shaun steps up to the bar to order some food and a drink while I consider my options. I decide to just have a drink for the time being. I walk up to the bar to order the drink that I instinctively order when flying, or when it's nine in the morning but it feels like four in the afternoon three days from now—a Bloody Mary. I pull up a stool and place my order. While the bartender gets to work I take a look around the room. It's a small place and it's early, but there are quite a few people sitting at the bar along with me.

At a table directly behind me is a soldier dressed in his desert camouflage, sitting quietly. A middle-aged man and woman are seated next to me. They have apparently formed a temporary bond over the fact that they are both traveling and are both employed by a business. The man looks to me like he might be named Edgar. The woman looks like a Colleen. I have no idea what their names actually are, but for the purposes of this story these are the names I will give them. The bartender hands me my drink and I sip it while idly eavesdropping on Edgar and Colleen's continuing discussion on the rigors of business travel. I look up at the television with little expectation, but to my surprise I see that CNN is reporting breaking news. The screen flashes and the expensive-looking graphics explode into place while words appear announcing the story. The thick haze that time difference and travel have clouded my brain with seem to clear instantly. Twenty-four Iraqi civilians have allegedly been murdered by American Marines in Haditha, Iraq.

Before even one word of the story is reported, Edgar says, "I don't believe that for a second. Those people were born hating us!"

It seems they've found something else they have in common because Colleen immediately exclaims, "Don't even get me started! I know exactly what you mean! I have a friend who has a kid over there right now!"

As they launch into a discussion about the intense and bizarre hate that Iraqis have for America, CNN cuts to an interview with a twelve-year-old Iraqi girl who is saying that she watched American soldiers come into her house and shoot her entire family. She says that she lived through the shooting by lying on the floor and pretending to be dead. I try to keep in mind that all of this is just alleged. All the facts aren't out yet, no one knows the whole story. But this is truly horrifying and I feel there is little to no likelihood that the girl is fabricating all of this. The report goes on to say that a few months ago the twenty-four dead were reported to have been killed by an IED (improvised explosive device). After some time passed, an article in *Time* magazine was released that told another story. The article contained many eyewitness accounts from Iraqis in Haditha who said they saw Marines invading homes and killing families after a roadside bomb killed a member of their platoon. The *Time* article prompted further investigation by the military. The investigators have concluded there was a cover-up but won't say if it is limited to the handful of Marines who did the killing. The investigation is ongoing and it could be weeks or months before any charges are brought.

Edgar and Colleen continue their conversation completely unaffected. According to what I overhear, the war is going along quite nicely, but the liberal media and the ungrateful, hateful Iraqis are trying to paint another picture. The soldier behind me, who I would imagine has been to Iraq, and is within earshot of the conversation, continues to sit quietly. Either he's not paying attention, or he's just listening and saying nothing. I can't help but wonder what he is thinking about all of this.

As I continue listening to the discussion beside me, and begin to really consider the statement that Edgar made the instant the story broke, I get more and more angry. He doesn't believe it for a second!!!?? Those people were born hating us!!??? Those people!!?? He immediately dismissed the allegations without even listening to one shred of evidence! Not only that, he dismissed it all based on the asinine notion that Iraqis are born hating us! I clench my teeth and begin to do what I always do when I'm incredibly angry. I imagine a scenario in which I express myself clearly and precisely to the object of my anger, with more conviction and articulation than I could possibly possess. I lay out all the facts plain and simple, and when I'm through, that person knows that they are completely and utterly wrong, and so does everyone around them. In reality I just sit there thinking about it all and saying nothing. I'm all too aware of the idiocy of this fantasy to ever try to make it a reality. I pick up the remainder of my Bloody Mary and join my friend Shaun at the table he's found.

All through the next few hours at the airport and the flight home I can't help thinking about the Haditha story and the things Edgar said. The idea of these soldiers from our country killing these families in cold blood makes me feel so much sadness, anger, and confusion. The thought of this man being able to brush all of it aside almost makes me feel worse. I dwell on it all for quite a while, just going in circles, until slowly my emotional response gives way to a more contemplative one. I begin to think about the way that Colleen immediately agreed with what Edgar said. I think about all of the people who would agree with him. There are so many people in our country who truly believe that people in Iraq hate us for no good reason and that the media is full of leftist fanatics bent on destroying our heroic president. I contemplate why people might think that things are so simple, as completely black and white as all that. It dawns on me that so many of them are probably doing exactly what Edgar did. They are immediately dismissing, or intentionally avoiding, every bit of information that doesn't coincide with their point of view.

Just as I start to become completely enraged at the willful and proud ignorance of conservative Americans everywhere, I have a realization. This is not something that only pro-war Republicans are guilty of. Anti-war liberals ignore and avoid information that contradicts their beliefs just as much. There are countless people on the left who think in the same simplistic, black-and-white ways, but believe the exact opposite of the people on the right. In fact, it begins to seem to me that anyone who is completely devoted to any cause or ideology is guilty of purposely ignoring evidence that is contrary to their beliefs. I suppose it's not really a new or startling revelation, but many times the realizations we have are not groundbreaking, they are just things that we've always known but never fully comprehended.

I start to think about all the different groups of people all over the world that are convinced that what they believe is absolute and nothing that anyone can say or do will change that. So many people with so many different, deeply held beliefs, and all of them convinced that they are the only ones who know the right answers. How many people are sustaining this faith through willful ignorance? Truthfully, I don't think it's ever been easier to do than it is today. There is a television station, radio station, Web site, and countless books catering to just about any ideology that anyone wants to embrace. We can immerse ourselves in a seemingly endless variety of information that will never contradict anything we have decided is true.

I can't help thinking about all of the various conflicts around the world that could be resolved if everyone were more open to the idea that they might be wrong. It all seems so simplistic and naive that I almost feel silly for thinking it. There must be something that I'm not taking into account. I consider that maybe if no one believed that they were completely right that no one would believe in anything at all and we'd all be lost and hopeless. But I immediately reconsider this. Being open to the fact that you might be wrong is not the same as not believing in anything. We can believe what we do because we've done our best to look at all the facts, considered things from all possible angles and then drawn our own conclusions. We can believe in these conclusions but still be aware that something or somebody might be able to show us another side of things that we hadn't previously seen. It seems to all be pretty reasonable to me. I guess the naive part is thinking that everyone could somehow be capable of, or willing to think like this.

There's an old saying that goes, "There are three sides to every story—your side, my side, and the right side." It's kind of a simple, humorous statement, but in most cases it's true. As I really start to think about that idea, I understand that it even applies to the alleged events in Haditha. Even if the initial reports are correct and it turns out that these Marines are guilty of murder, there will be another side of the story that I would have never considered in my initial reaction. There is the story of confused kids who were taught to kill and then thrown into the middle of life-and-death situations and expected to make the right decisions every day. The men in charge of them equally confused on how to lay out clear guidelines for the war being fought. It's a complicated story that will in no way exonerate these soldiers, but it is nonetheless extremely important that I not ignore it. It dawns on me that it's in no way any less important than it was for Edgar not to ignore the story of the Iraqi people that morning. In my own way I was doing the same thing that he did. Even though I didn't ignore the story, I still made up my mind without hearing all of it. I don't want to make my conclusions based on my emotional responses, and I don't want to be like so many people in the world who find the political party, news show, or religion that most closely mirrors their own beliefs and then take everything they say as fact. I want to do my best to find out what is truly right, and I think that the only way to do that is to always keep in mind that I might be wrong.

**SHAWN HARRIS**
The Matches

## *My Doe*

by first snow
by first snow my Doe
ought to have a ring
Lord I—I been saving
but Hope is on a rope
Hope's on a frayed rope
and I can count her ribs
from our kitchenette window

I'm scared and unprepared
she's startin to show

when we found Hope
when we brought home Hope
last of the litter down the way
the cataract in her right eye cloudy grey
we never said
never said, but both knew
adopting her meant more
than any ceremony her mama's waiting for

I'm scared and unprepared
she's startin to show

my Doe's a little bit psycho
but she look all right with the lights low
my Doe wear her head inside out
my Doe know that I don't mind though
my Doe
my Dear
my female
she sell
retail
by the
C
V
S
pharmacy store.

Shawn Harris

**RYAN TRASTER**

Small Towns Burn a Little Slower

## Death Rattle

I was sent to this desert with no bread or water, just a guitar in hand. The sun beaming down on my skin as I crawled deeper into the sand. I sang "all my life I've needed someone else, now I'm just happy with myself. I won't try to take back anything I've done, because I was just having fun."

So I sit in this state with a smile on my face, as the vultures circle my head. Think of the times that others made me cry and I laugh, thinking, all this time it didn't matter in the end, the people I've let down or couldn't seem to impress. Wasting my life trying to live for someone else. When all that mattered was myself.

**JON TUMMILLO**
Folly

### *This Is Exactly What It Doesn't Feel Like to Be in Space*

Door.
Awake.
The first and second word.
Addressing stranglers.
A Film adjacent the lips.
Adhesive warnings.
Dawn is quite the confident prick.
Human lasagna.
Furiously unhinge the jaw.
Porch swing in a thunderstorm.
In present tense.
Intense Presence.
Neglect as a cancer.
Flying coach.
Instruct the coasts to share the cost.
Hire, fuck, and fire secretaries.
In a lifetime of conceptions, never and none.
Wind.
Relate.
Knows everyone by heart.
The battle of breath.

Gavels pelting hung jurists.
Force-feeding the fed.
Stenographers cutting corners.
Hand-me-down pendant.
Heirlooms and oral traditions.
Giants winning the penance.
Generations.
Taking, giving.
Earth drugs itself solemn.
Tranquil strides.
Advise a starving magician.
To hire, fuck, and fire rabbits.
In a lifetime of conclusions, never and none.

**GABE SAPPORTA**
Cobra Starship

## *Success*

Has its price
Can you hear me now
That I'm dumbing myself down
Am I filling you with doubt
That I am
Who you thought?

I know it's just a game
But I'm playing it to win
I won't forget from where I came
But it's time to take over
It's over

I'm tired of waiting
So tired of waiting
I'm tired of being the
Poor
Cliché
Misunderstood

### *It's Warmer in the Basement*

You can't escape now
I've got you locked inside this room
You know I tip good
And soon, you will love me too

Don't be upset now
You know I get angry too
Don't make me hurt you
It's true:
No one hears you in this room

This is what you get when you're talking back baby
I never bounce a check so give it up baby.
Open up your eyes
I want to watch you cry
Come on, come on
The camera's on

Now I'm a changed man
But as a boy I was so true
The world can't protect you
Not like money will

You want some bread now?
Just promise me

You'll never make me believe
    it's true
No one hears you in this room

## JOE BROWN

### *Lola and Gus*

Embody me,
Heal my aching emptiness.
Render me,
Captive upon grief.
Agony,
My maiden's withering.
Envy me,
Roaming wild inside her heart.
Sorrow,
A curse I long to distance.
Hinder me,
Useless against her aching.

Fantasies expire with my spirit,
The battle between the Holy and Hell,
Divine behind green eyes,
A solace sleeper with blond hair,
A vivid scar becomes my heart,
A pale face struggles with tears.

Depart me,
And revealed is the object of my affection.

## STEVE CHOI
Rx Bandits

### *Purge*

Hurt me! Give me pain to see the truth because comfort gets
me nowhere.
I become gross.
Mind polluted, the very essence of my being has been diluted.
Objectify less! Feel more, then I'll stop feeling like such a whore.
But I still want more!
Shift my desires, stabilize the mind.
Seek self-worth of a different kind.
Hold the face that fronts the mind that represents the soul that
hides the past
that taints the future that repeats the problem.
It's the pronoun that brings you down when things get
complicated,
which longs for simplicity that forgets hectic behavior which
needs to rest
when we need to wake up.
Calm down.

## *Blah*

Light me! Burn the burn that hates to love to live to play.

Crazy! The life so loud that won't show the way.

In confusion surrender, in despair reach out, in triumph forget what good is about.

These are the things that procreate, centered in a self that's easy to hate.

Soul, I love you for leading me well. Mind, you are wonderful for executing the passions of the heart.

Self . . . you still need to put these things together.

You have far to go but it's been getting better.

Live the life you want to live, give all the things that you can give.

So many layers, afraid of getting cold, but you better learn to stay warm

before you get old.

We must believe our hearts are true.

I practice, I fail, but will push through.

## MATT EMBREE
Rx Bandits

Well it's coming down to it
on the air raid siren
would you hold my hand
as the rockets hit the ground
with a silent melancholy
'til it's too bright to see
would you sit with me here
while the grass is still green?

(_____) is the inevitable failure of will, the wink eyed seductress
in a wispy white blouse all dance and flirt, confident, secure yet
aloof and shallow. She is undoubtedly blond, skipping around
in circles, arms outstretched, skin ablaze and of silk, smooth and
supple, fleeting and furtive. You try to gather her up all over
you, feel her drip down your thighs, bunching her dress around
her waist in a fervent, maddening series of thrusts, her teeth on
your neck and ears, her breath moist and hot, her voice like
explosions of magma from red-lipped volcano. She pulls and
claws at your flesh, stripping skin and sinew 'til backbone is
exposed and raw, veins bloated to burst. You build a mountain
of your own and climb atop it and holding breath you leap
from your body and erupt inside her, soul and structure,
pouring and flooding, deluge of freedom, idealist's revolt,
beginning of eternity, slumping into flat lifeless amoeba with a

slurp and a gurgle, stuck to second hand, servant of gnats and slug alike, a fly on a swatter, fried cheese on the spatula. As quick as the onset she is gone, the bites and stings and handfuls of satin a daydream, not a scar nor a drop of blood, fingers and genitals dry as desert, blank as brand-new canvas of artist or first page of poet. And then the ache, the onset of eye-bulge, disbelief, remorse, regret, self-degradation. She has left you not as she met you but rather as wraith, specter, undead minion of the half-living, servant of remorse, reproach and regret.


we are so eager to brand ourselves
with someone else's words
so sing me not your politics
you know we've heard it all before
your tried and true philosophy
old clothes wrapped in plastic
we're still searching for a meaning,
an exclusive destination
to define us a beginning
and explain it at the end
now we overlook the middle
and all that is now living
squares of glass for looking
covet, but do not touch
instead we numb the feeling
and carve out deep the present word
scribble down the theme songs
of adverts in between the talk show hosts

sing me not your education
your so-called scholars worth
much more there is to be written down
than that which may be trapped with pen and paper

**BOBBY DARLING**

Gatsbys American Dream

## *The Museum*

I can shift the ideas around like tectonic plates in my dreams, creating a super continent where I'll find you. It's been tens of millions of years but I'll come back for you, I'll dig in the rocky ground of my brain until I find your bones. I can see the nape of your neck and the curvature of your spine so clearly in my mind, I can feel you and smell you and see the things you did. I study your body like a fossil, and I imagine you developing wings for taking flight in the sky. I brush the pebbles from your bones, gently, so gently. I carefully remove millions of years of debris from your remains to recreate your graceful form in my head. How fragile you were, fragile and delicate and unable to cope with the rapid climate change inside of my world. So I'll rebuild your skeleton and keep it for all time in my museum, where I can gaze upon your frame with love and adoration.

## M. S. BREEN
`Emanuel`

with your legs spread and mouth waxed.
you're bleached out by the sun.
your eyes look like drainpipes.
when your mascara runs, away.

always surrounded by the salt of the earth.
a nervous dance with a liar.
when can I see you again?
and set you on fire.

need you.
burn you.
skin you.
wear you.

call you.
want you.
fold you.
tear you.

anathema sweetheart,
with a dead aim to please.
but can you trust these days,
always down on your knees?

you're all aesthetics and no milk.
a sad fashion queen.
we'll watch you soak up the limelight.
we'll watch you deep throat a dream.

love you.
chase you.
fuck you.
share you.

need you.
feel you.
lose you.
dare you.

### my anapex.

turn me on, the way old friends do.
you disappear and I would die to follow you.
suck my blood, like all great lovers do.
oh when we kiss I feel the disease, your heart's vacuum.

(blow her out like smoke
with a somatic cough.
she dissipates in the air,
it's over now when I exhale)

crash my car. I'll be your abandonment star.
cripple me and I will crawl back in your jar.

(blow her out like smoke
with a late night phone call.
she dissipates in the air,
it's over now when I exhale)

**AARON BARRETT**

Reel Big Fish

## *Tastes Like Christmas*

marvelous madness surrounds this ten fingered ball of exploding
universes and alligator shavings

is that the flames of hell and the devil on a jet ski i see in the
sparkling blue waters of her tropical paradise eyes
she talks the armadillos out of their aftershave avalanches
and makes the cattle prod doctors burst into tearful sawdust
operas
she kicks the shins and breaks the skin with teeth of gentle
catastrophe
i should be so lucky as to have my burnt chocolate chip cookie
of a heart dipped in such a cool glass of milk money nose bleeds
to lose a digit in that spinning saw blade of beautiful bone
crushing smiles would be too much dreaming for day and night
combined and combed over like bald men or corn on the cob
destiny or the fried slices of my birthday cake and the melted
candles of a wish finally granted
who believes in this stuff anyway
a not so poetic reflection for a girl that is absolute perfection

**ADAM TURLA**

## *Spring #1*

I watch from across state lines
her long fingers
clip roots of weeds
scurry through the dirt
help pumpkin seeds push upwards

she has springtime skin
face shines— Is that all?
Are her eyes bluer? Lips brighter?
No, nothing has changed.

That sun shows its dinner plate face
for a few days and
out come the tank tops!
Ticker tape! High school marching bands!

## CHRIS FRANGICETTO
### Days Away

1.

we live in shadow, we grow immune
hopeful of becoming whole again
can these deceptions be overcome?
will what's missing ever be found?
time is inanimate, yet we exist here.


a memory awakes a forgotten feeling . . .


feeding this fire, keep it alive
if we set it free, all is lost
than alone and in the dark again
where deep thoughts run wild.


2.

happy is a point of view, up and down coexist, but I'll never
give up being real, tell me . . . was there a point to us? you see
my name and think of a random proverb, I can't do that again
for some reason. As one person goes . . . so shall we all, trained
like animals to follow in suit, make up your mind, use it as it
uses me, it's easy to assume I lost because I didn't win, I came
out of a dream and forgot to bring my mind with me. I know
you know me. How do you feel?

3.

When my bones are frozen, sentences will never be completed. Alone is a feeling that is a disease. It must be stopped. Love is a naive pimp, and anxiety its coldhearted whore. One of you can inch closer, and I wouldn't oppose. True I am, but what you know is not always the same as what you see. A lost faith in another is always hard to overcome. A syringe in many ways is like romance. It carries you away, deceptively heaven, then it doesn't let go, and soon our dream pops just like the balloon.

4.

falling isn't easy, I never felt pain before this, clamps on my hands, these shoes cannot go where I need to, must take a chance, fear is near, minutes—hours it all means nothing, give me a moments silence and I'll repay my debt, arms of passion, thoughts of her, crowds are for fakes, hidden in my sleep—are all my demons waiting there for me?
clear as the ocean looming in the night, my life is. so uncertain are things I once took to be natural. laughable my thoughts are, cant even connect anymore. wanted memories become unwanted ones, keeping myself together with scotch tape is fun. a new window . . . could u open it? I know you're not afraid, I'll be on my way now. Lines are for beggars. make me smile again. inclined to do so as is the will of others. in my hands everything was so good: even the worst times were the best. Leap of faith. what is faith?

5.

the stretch marks on my soul keep expanding . . . the capacity amazes even me sometimes. I live for you all, not a thought about my own wishes. death would never strike fear into the hearts of men of my design. what is one more gravity bong hit . . . why not, I ask u? giving in, is what we do best these days.

A drink over good conversation is never a bad thing.

I'll be sleeping alone tonight, how many times will I repeat this process over the next week, the next month, let's try and not make a habit of it.

fight to win.

I'll do my best to revive u, but will you keep me waiting long? it's dark and I'm lost . . . meet mr. ignorance, he will show you the way. hang on to what you've got, or it will die like everything else.

6.

my dreams are crowded as of late
sounds of demons returning to their origin
wearing fake clothes doesn't cut it anymore
originality is seeping from holes in my spine
incomplete wrongs, and yet created similar
A deluge of pain and haunting desires
formidable is this foe i stand alone to face
A clean slate, I won't stray from my goal
time bleeds from stress just like we all do

Care to share a lesson, I too spilled the coffee
plans wont change the living on days like this
darkness always comes from behind your back
leaping into a bottle solves all my problems
Loneliness is coming down the street

The child inside forgets what he once saw
Mirrors show the capacity of a man's lust
don't hold on to something that's proven to grumble
the hearts of man are as confusing as they come
hurt is a capricorn these days? not likely

Structure or happiness . . . no way is safe
blocks of desperation feel strangely comfortable
death, is it living inside of us all?
My feet wear what magic I have left,
Don't order me around, I keep what I kill
If they are too cunning, learn to hunt better.
I'll leave you where I found you.

## STEVE ELKINS

The Autumns

## *One Central Fire Against Two Craters: Part One*

When one of the boys places a rock in my hand, I have an unexpected flash of memory. A Bollywood actress in an ornate turquoise sari walking in slow motion through a cow pasture, like Radha toward her Krishna, pupils rippling with emerging tears. Then a voiceover: "Rani, the actress, tells me that where she comes from they say there is no difference between God and a stone." The surfacing of this memory can probably be attributed to the fact that both the boy and I are aware that the identity of this object as a rock is incidental. What he has left in my open palm is a language. A skeleton key. An instrument that has been known to make a sound that penetrates deaf ears. He knows that when it leaves my hand to trace its arc, this otherwise unremarkable object, which only two days before could still be identified as part of a wall in a home, will sink like karma into the flesh that reduced it to rubble. About a hundred pairs of eyes are waiting expectantly. I am surrounded and I've lost sight of Vikrum. One boy speaks what has remained unspoken: "Stop the bulldozers."

When I met Vikrum on a bus to Dharamsala, where the Dalai Lama lives spearheading the Tibetan government-in-exile on the slopes of the lower Himalayas, I could not have predicted that our friendship would result in my being asked to lead a riot in the biggest slum in Asia. Back then, navigating through goats and children on the boulder-strewn slopes, through occasional small villages of terraced green fields drowning in mustard flowers on the way to the snow line, Vikrum told me about the work he was doing in Bombay, educating children in the slums and teaching self-esteem classes. Knowing I would eventually be flying home from Bombay, he invited me to crash at his apartment there for a couple days before leaving. I asked if I could accompany him to the slums to meet his students, many of which were from villages in some of the bleakest regions of India I had visited earlier in the trip. With lacerated optimism, I hoped that this would provide some long overdue counterpoint of good things happening in very dark places.

When I arrived on his doorstep two weeks later, he was visibly shaken. "Two days ago," he explained, "a slum that many of my students live in was bulldozed in an effort to clean up the city. Two-thirds of my students are now completely homeless, have not shown up to class since, and I'm beginning to doubt I'll ever see them again." Thanks to the caste system, life in India is a lottery, so the people are already pretty acclimated to the idea that an opportunity to go to school is like possessing a winning ticket, a luxury rather than a right. Vikrum knew that as "untouchables" most of his students would be sent back to their rural villages to live the rest of their lives in near primitive conditions, lives of backbreaking manual labor and appalling poverty, especially for the women, who do the same work for half the wages in a culture already conducive to rampant domestic abuse. The day I arrived was the first day Vikrum had mustered enough courage to visit the aftermath in hopes of finding some of his students. He would try to convince the parents to keep them in school, as it would be their only hope of getting the kids out of the slums, and if nothing else, Vikrum hoped to offer some feeble words of encouragement and a farewell.

After helping teach the class lessons in English and math, I accompanied Vikrum and his remaining students home. Initially, we were stopped by representatives from the demolition company who wouldn't let us through.

"These are our students," Vikrum protests. "We are walking them home to their families."

"No one lives here anymore," we are told. Another teacher from the school is with us, and is trying to reach the head of the demolition company and city officials on her cell phone. Meanwhile, we try a more concealed route through the claustrophobic alleys of the slum dwellings, dodging rats, cockroaches, and exposed live wires that dangle murderously at head level, until we emerge into what looks like nothing short of a war zone.

I had expected to see a block or two of makeshift homes flattened into the mud. Instead, what I saw looked as if a militia of suicide bombers had run through a city center. I walked into a landscape of rubble that stretched all the way to the high-rises in the distant city skyline. Hundreds of people, many of them children, were sifting through the debris for their belongings, occasionally pulling out a tattered piece of clothing or a toy they recognized. They navigate between scattered columns of smoke. Vikrum starts climbing over the wreckage to look for familiar faces alongside the river of raw sewage at its margin.

This is a confirmed malaria black spot, so I try to keep moving fast to avoid the mosquitoes, constantly slipping and causing landslides of debris that leave gashes on my skin even through my jeans. Vikrum is scrambling across the chaos to a little girl he has recognized. A small group of boys has surrounded me, seemingly incredulous that a westerner is walking through their neighborhood and all at once they begin heaping questions on me about America and what it is like. It feels demoralizing for me to give answers. After six weeks in India, America has already begun to feel like nothing more than an idea. So I try to redirect things with questions of my own.

"How long have you lived here?"

"Twenty-five years."

"Did they give you any forewarning?"

"Two days."

"Did anyone try to resist?"

"What could we do? Every family was told they would receive some rupees. No one has seen any money."

"Where will you go?"

Numb silence. No one has any idea of course. They wouldn't be living in the slum if they had somewhere else to go.

I search for Vikrum. He is holding the hands of two little girls he knows as he walks with them to find their parents. We spot more of his students along the way. One of the girls takes us to her mom and three siblings who have constructed a temporary structure of garbage bags on tree branches. Having just salvaged a pot out of a small mountain of wreckage, the mother offers to make me a cup of chai while she tries to stop the bleeding of her five-year-old's foot, which had been split open from having to walk in this environment without shoes. Flies fleck their faces between dangling clumps of unwashed hair. Although Vikrum is playing patty-cake with some of the girls in an effort to make them remember another life, he has become very quiet and there is a dark glaze over his eyes. This makes me especially worried. He does not seem to be teetering between shock and emotional collapse. Familiarity and time appear to have placed him far beyond their reach. I'm afraid he's sinking into apathy.

The boys I talked to earlier keep following me and their group becomes increasingly bigger. Then something happens that, in my mind, illustrates a fundamental difference between my reality and theirs: as I stare in horror at the approach of two new bulldozers coming directly toward us, most people seem to be more interested in me, even though clusters of people are gathering behind the machines, picking up debris and any other projectiles they can pilfer along the way. Everyone seems to be waiting for someone else to throw first.

That was when a rock was placed in my hands.

I'm in a state of shellshock, so the older boys react for me: they begin pushing me toward the bulldozer until I am standing directly in front of it. They are chanting in my support. I get the impression they believe I will evoke some magical authority of the West, or at least of cinema, and awake them from the nightmare of their history. The other teacher puts down her cell, realizing the irrelevance of getting an official on the line given the momentum of this pivotal moment, and shouts fiercely to as many people as can hear her, "If you want a riot, I will lead it! Just give me some confirmation that this is what you really want and I will throw the first stone!" I take advantage of this distraction and step out of the way. The crowd is getting bigger and closing in on the bulldozers but still no one is doing anything. Finally, a young kid throws something and then there are five, then ten people throwing rocks and debris at the men inside the steel frames. The drivers react by changing course to speed erratically toward the attackers who disperse like mosquitoes. The female teacher, who is now the only one fixed on retaliation, is shouting: "Don't you want this? Why don't you fight?! You have to stand up for yourselves!!" Someone yells back what everyone is secretly thinking: "What do you think that will actually accomplish?"

And it is over as quickly as it began.

In stark contrast to what I had seen in Latin America three months prior, I discovered that India is a place where most people are utterly resigned to their poverty. The culture fosters it. It's built into their religion.

It doesn't take long for a crowd to surround me again. Now they are openly mocking me in Hindi and Bihari. "Look guys, the American has an eye booger!" to the hilarity of all. A fuse has been blown in my processing capacity but I know that their dignity has just been dealt a serious blow. Unsure how to direct their residual anger, others begin beating each other up, right in front of me.

I hear Vikrum calling me. He motions for me to get away from the crowd, but they follow me. When I get closer, he says, "Stand here, next to these women," gesturing toward a little girl and her teenage sister. When I do so, I turn to find that the crowd seems to be caught in an invisible net. "Men are scared to death of women in this country," he suggests. "They are raised to have almost no interaction with them until they are married . . ." He pauses as if debating whether to complete the thought. "And that is a big part of why this country is so fucked up."

For a moment, we are unsure what to say to each other and simply survey the strange planet we find ourselves standing on. Then he adds, "You know, the guys who drive the bulldozers . . . they live in slums too. They probably know some of the families who came out to stop them. In a way, the people inside the bulldozers were fighting for the same thing as the people who attacked them."

But maybe, I should start from the beginning . . .

## DANIEL BARRON
Dollar Fifty Date

## *Purgatory at the Jersey Shore*

Daylight is breathing over the skyline,
On the drive home, somewhere past three a.m.,
Eight hours on the road, billboards read like lullabies,
This engine is singing me asleep behind the wheel.

As I awoke to the song of seagulls,
I open the driver's door and wander across the street,
To hear the percussion of waves crashing upon the shore,
I whisper, "This is so surreal."

I walk past the lifeguard's tall wooden station,
It's knocked over into the cloudy beach,
Following the sounds of the ocean,
I make my way to the shoreline.

My feet sink into the wet sand,
As liquid glass washes over my heels,
In a trance, I see a boy donned in black clothing,
He wades into the water, wading on until he sinks through
the sea.

I realize I'm not breathing,
As I light my cigarette and take three long drags,

The boy emerges from the depths,
To tell me that he didn't drown.

Suddenly, it all comes back to me,
I see the accident that took my life,
Like a terrible dream,
I can feel the windshield smashed against my face.

A man with tattoo-covered arms runs by,
He doesn't even give a glance at me.

I fear I am a ghost, oh my,
I'm invisible and silent to the world.

I cannot feel the wind as it blows against my arms,
Walking across this desert by the sea,
I brush my hair out of my eyes,
To see this beachside town is purgatory.

Exactly as one would think,
Neither damning, nor enlightening,
Neither white, nor black, just grey,
It's a nice sight, yet nothing worthy of a painting.

I climb the stairs to the boardwalk,
Sitting in a nearby bench, a mother and child,
As I pass, the baby starts to cry,
How can he see me, so invisible?

I take a seat upon the railing,
To wait and watch the rising sun,
As it lifts the clouds and parts the sky,
And reflects rays off of the ocean.

The light is so bright it's blinding. I close my eyes.
The warmth of the sun kisses my cheeks,
and the wind embraces my face,
I open my eyes.

**JERRY JONES**
Trophy Scars

## Jerry and Jerry Go for a Drive

Hey, kid? You there?
Yeah!? How you feeling today?
"Ok" Just "Ok?" "Ok" is good enough for me. C'mon! Let's go!
Get in the car
Don't worry, it's not cold out, actually you would agree—it's
quite nice
Windows down. Remember the rules?
Of course you do!

How old are you today? Twenty-two?
No? Ten?
No? What is it?
Six?
Six it is then.
What's been keeping you locked up in there? Up in there—up
inside that place no one sees?
I haven't seen you in a while, man. You all right?

I know it's snowing out.
Don't worry though. It's warm, I swear.
You see? Not so bad, right?

No, we won't drive so fast. But you have to remember the rules.
Yeah, heh, I still smoke, funny, we both smoke still. Thought we
were gonna quit years ago.

So what's up?
What's going on with your head, little guy?
Broken bones? Can't sleep? Bad stomach, again? What is it? Are
there manta rays in your pool?
Ah, I see. Well, that's a little more complicated.
Look, once time is initiated—
I mean once it really starts, you can't stop it.
Not only can't you stop it, but it goes really fast.
Oh shiii— . . . Hold on, here comes a turn!

Sorry, I forgot about that turn. Always sneaks up on me.
Hey, but it's beautiful out, huh? Snowing like hell but it's sunny
and it's gotta be like seventy-five
degrees!
Right, right. Back to time. Well she's leaving you.
There's just nothing you can do about it. You watched this
happen before.
She has nothing left to tell you. She's tired of explaining. You're
exhausting her.
She's not yours! Never was. She really did a number on us, Jer.
I know. I know. I'm dying about it too! It's not your fault. But
what are you gonna do?
Tell her "no"? Ask her to come back? You definitely can't stop her.
You can't stop time and she needs to go. Everyone needs to go.

Let's get to the comic book store—that makes you feel better, right?

No? Last time I checked—we loved comics when we were six, huh? No?

I know, little man. It's gonna hurt forever. Remember, I know.
I know you. You know me. Have a smoke.
Pop in your favorite record, Jer. C'mon. One that you love.
You can't remember what you love?
That's the problem, man.
I can't, until you can.
I miss you, Jerry Jones.

**BRANDON RIKE**
Dead Poetic

## We Are Vultures

I saw it breathe its last breath,
And cower and shrink to the floor.
In those seconds after
I saw, in vain, it gasp for more.
Here from this perch
I watched them all
Lose their lives one by one.
And I sat here watching it,
'Til the last trace of life was gone.
Upon this rotting faithful branch
I watch five corpses become decay.
Waiting for the perfect chance
To feed off the remains.
See, we are the luckiest.
The cunning that survive.
No, we were the faithful-est.
Its death has brought us life.
We stay here, perched to watch you die
Watching each step of your life turn
Your death will let us thrive.
We're the faithful—the Vultures,
And we are still alive.

**NICK MARTIN**
Underminded

## I'm committed to safe driving

stoned.
watching fluttered rooftops; the eyes, the wings of an illiterate saint.
questioned.
as part of the eyes that I cannot see. as tender as lips eluded in foreign dialect.
oh, and don't forget your home is where you felt it.
engulfed by the salty floods. shooting your mouth is not abrasive.
shallow as you. in open lakes behind elder trees.
the eldest consumer bought in with the dream.
sailing. and open arms to the precious awakening.
eluded again.
eluded once.

## Drugs VS. The Patriot VS. Paris

As if the women spoke in tongues, while preaching about white
mirage in coated cacophony.
Desired by few less than the hollowed cavities; in design,
tidiness in speculation
And you think your drugs are better than the shepherds?

The patriot versus paris.

Alas! The bigot has risen from nine days sleep, just in time for
the moon to burn these pores.
Red dirt versus paris; and you doubted a betrayal between "the
harp" and "the ox."

Chuckle and point and stare and bless and spit on the tides.

A cheap fuck is worth every penny if everyone is buying in.
Remember what I said about patriots and paris?
You're not understanding the routine the patriot severs by
listening to YOU!
Exploring the children's blasphemic symphonies, and putting
your ears to the door; in hopes of hearing your shitty fate no
one cares about anymore.

You are not serving an understanding that the routine severs
the listening of the patriot in yourself.

Your drugs were better when you weren't yourself. When they were me. When I was your drug and choices.

Call it what you wish to name it in stupid, anonymous canoes.
Onto your petty game about "oxes."
Cold fellows with no cash to hand off to Mr. answers.
Azariah and his terrible addictions to life and razor thick lines.
I . . . . . . fucked . . . . . . something.
'N that something fucks me too.
Even you can't open your eyes to see what I say!

Cocaine is spelled in the great american sob story.

**EVAN JEWETT**
`Worker Bee`

*loss of a squirt gun—*

i squint like a child
looking up at the sun
it floats down to me

lions are resting
down on the street
having had enough, the flowers grow feet

i lift up your head
and look for the fleas
they welcome their purpose

all the while
when i wasn't looking
the lions got a little closer

## lost keys—

i sang a song of your beauty in cruel mocking form
cracking the high notes that fell out of their nest
muting the strings of your hair

i painted your arms to your chair
looking up to the sky i bit my lips
and gave orion a suit of gold

i hugged your neck and thought of work
you came in through the window
so i closed the door

conner family moneymaking death machine—

turn on the moneymaking death machine
the dark turns to grey
results appear quickly and not soon enough

the all knowing, all giving, all loving
moneymaking death machine

millions of people don't know they are happy
until their machine is on
and they can see it grinding away

what would our bones look like as dust?
how would they smell?

bye bye sweet highs and lows
make way for the middle ground
it promises you pleasant, so turn it on and walk away

**DUANE OKEN**

`Socratic`

## *Honorable Discharge*

The rain dripping down the awnings down into my driveway is always a familiar noise. Even when I was little it annoyed me. How I could hear it hit the roof, then fall into all the holes that make up the driveway. That driveway creeps me out. I get awoken some nights from footsteps casually walking up it.

They belong to a Vietnam vet. If only he served his country as much as he served his liver. He stumbled his way up that concrete almost every single night. I could smell his cheap cigars as he passed my window. With the night behind him, he would go to the basement that he called home and shut his eyes.

His eyes have probably seen things that I can't even imagine. Things that no one should. There was a night when he came home plastered and sat down in a chair to rub alcohol on his injured leg. After three puffs of his cigar he fell asleep. The cigar dropped and his body slowly caught fire along with the rest of the basement.

I bet he thought he would die from an enemy bullet and not from being an alcoholic. I feel the war led him to drink as much as he did. So in a way it did kill him. I still get awoken from footsteps on the driveway at night. They're not as loud and the cigar smell is not as strong but I still notice them. I guess some people can't handle certain things. But then again I guess sometimes there are things that no one can handle.

**NICK THOMAS**
The Spill Canvas

## Galaxy Eater

I'm a slave to these words—I am shackled to my verbs . . .
From my nose to my shoes, I swallow galaxies for you—
anything to lift that spirit of yours . . .
My mouth dripping wet with sin down my chin—tell me where
do I end and where do you begin?

## ERIC VICTORINO
`Strata`

### *Stray Bullet Effect*

Yes,
it is a small, small world.
and the damn thing
is shrinking fast.

they talk about butterflies
fluttering their wings in remote tropical forests—
but now it's more like
a punch-up drunk at a bar,
a stray bullet fired while you wait for a bus
swerving to avoid debris in the road,
smashed by a semi-truck
or spinning out of control across
six lanes of speed—

a dirty look can get you killed.
simple misunderstandings
can lead to murder,
the way we are today.

who knows?
maybe there really is

someone's mother somewhere
laying in a hospital bed
with a bum back
because you don't watch your step
on the sidewalk.

these days I don't think
there are many coincidences.

we're too close together.

## BRIAN TASCH
**Boy Armageddon**

tonight
it is you
and me
drowning
in a sea
of the cheapest wine
that love can buy
but relax
because romance
can be faked
so easily
when you've been drinking

**BOB NANNA**
The City on Film

This is what I do and it's awfully important. That will be the name of this particular interlude. It's fitting, as it's the very first thing I wrote into a notebook while on a plane somewhere above Colorado on January 30, 2006. There's no rhyme or reason to the inclusion of that particular passage, just as there's no rhyme or reason to the actual inception of it in the first place. I was probably upset. Worried about money. Worried about an upcoming eye doctor's appointment (which by the way revealed non-Hodgkin's lymphoma, which by the way has been treated, and which by the way is gone forever from my life). Or maybe I was just bored and passing time during a long cross-country flight. I don't recall 100% and, to be honest, that makes it especially interesting . . . to me. Words written and then forgotten. Forgotten words unearthed and taken way out of context. New context applied to old words. Fun for all.

So what follows is a random collection of various entries into various notebooks and journals over a good ten or so years. Even I am perplexed by some of it. I vaguely remember an episode in Norway where a tour mate exclaimed, "This is how we do it in New York!" as he went to intervene in a increasingly violent domestic disturbance. I can recreate the scene in my head as the aggressor took a look at him and yelled in broken English, "Who da fuck are you?!" Or given the amount of time since the incident, perhaps I'm embellishing. Perhaps that was the point. Write down only vague details. Make the story work . . . later.

I also sorta kinda remember starting work on a screenplay. The first scene took place at a train station. A romantic comedy? A black comedy? A political drama? A sci-fi musical? I don't remember. It's safe to say that eight years later, thank god, no film has been made. It was written and then forgotten about.

This fucking bin is overflowing with junk such as this. Some of it's okay and some of it eventually made its way into songs here and there. And then again, some of it (to quote Ricky Gervais) seems more likely to have been "written on a mental hospital wall in shit." So here goes. I've included dates and places when available. Good luck. We're all counting on you.


01/30/06:

This is what I do and it's awfully important. I'm drinking a Bloody Mary. A five-dollar Bloody Mary. What I do. It's so fucking important. When did I forget how to write? When did my flawless penmanship get so bad? When did the word *penmanship* get so hard to write? This is not important. Nothing in this book is important.

I will be asleep tomorrow. All day. It's inevitable. And it's much better this way. Both of us, we're passing time in our own ways. And here, up in this airplane, I am truly alone. Even more than I was in Bakersfield or those two nights when I slept in my car. I had a lifeline, truly. Someone could be there for me, if I needed.

Seven hundred and twenty-nine dollars for a fucking rental

car. Where does all this money go? What will happen tomorrow? Will I even be able to see? What kind of medicine are they going to throw my way? Has my ATM card been turned off? I wonder. Because it's not working. Goodnight.

Unknown, most likely 2005:

Not bad in terms of terrible. Not quite what I was waiting for. A quick wit with lack of narrative wins second place sash with Early Wynn's autograph. Alone in the union of Iowa U. Two hours with (crossed out) then hysteria in the cafeteria. A curious red wonder in the area. Hurry lemme see. Let's take a week off from everyone. (crossed out)

2/15/03, Allentown, PA:

Please allow me to be blunt yet painfully vague. That has never happened . . . but then again, maybe it has . . . in a painfully soft way. Remember Joseph? What exactly are you looking for here, son? How H must it be? I dunno. But here's what I do know. I've seen it time and time again. Rock collectors come in pairs . . . but these aren't rock collectors, dummy. Yes that's right. I'm in the rumbleseat. What a party that could've been.

11/30/01, Columbus, OH:

You have pain somewhere always. Traffic through the city. Wrist feeling a lot better. Strap problem fixed. Laundry finally done tonight. Brown guitar fixed. Scrabble 11 to 2. Great show yesterday. Finally, doctor. Lots of email. You like them. The thing about drinking beer in a car.

1/10/99, San Francisco, CA:

She's leaving. I'm sleeping in someone else's dirty room. Dirty bed. San Francisco. After the show, we could've talked, could've something. But you were so embarrassingly drunk. I couldn't even stand to be around you anymore. Kinda like you could hardly stand. I'm in Portland now and I used to like Storm & Stress.

11/20/98, Moss, Norway:

Andre the Lion, the punkers hittin me with a bottle, "sex and violence," man beating girlfriend, "This is how do it in New York," kicking papers, big fat Indian meal, dog humps Pete, me and a plate, bergen discussions.

10/26/98, Cleveland, OH:
Scene #1: The Machine Gun

BILLY: What are you carrying there?

JOE: Oh in this (case)? Pool cues. Yeah . . . I'm heading into the Loop for the . . . Chapstick Billiards Championship down at 8-Ball.

BILLY: Why in *that* case?

JOE: Well, y'know, I like to go in there all incognito and surprise the competition into thinking I'm just the entertainment for the night . . .

BILLY: (not buying it) Oh I see . . .

JOE: No, actually, I'm lying . . . It's a machine gun. Yeah. Ever see the movie *El Mariachi*?

BILLY: No.

JOE: Neither have I. Heard it's good though.

BILLY: I play guitar, too, you know. And I was a damn good bil-
liards player in my day.

JOE: Really? Do you have any experience with machine guns?

BILLY: Hmm . . . does laser tag count?

JOE: Absolutely.


10/24/98, Rochester, NY:

Make sure you tell her that you miss her.

## CRAIG OWENS
`Chiodos`

when i sleep, why do i have nightmares of children being hit
by cars and serial killers wearing buffalo heads at my family
reunions?

is it the same reason that when i am alone in my apartment i
set up the pillows on my bed to face the door, with my phone
in my hand, 911 already dialed.

when i look in the mirror, why do i spend hours staring at my
eyes, and not looking into them. ranting the 7 syllables of my
name over and over, sometimes for up to an hour or more.

and why is it that i spend so much time trying to figure out
why i should say things, when i should just be shouting them.

## JESSE KURVINK
`HelloGoodbye`

### *I love you and I miss you all the time*

all of those douglas firs,
trains, transformers, bluebirds.
anxious and my o.c.d.
cereal, atomic energy
and all the answers to everything;

tesla coils, decaffeinated tea
so much more put together than me.

the interstates and, the difference in weather;

i'm so glad you're there to put all my pieces back together.

**KELCEY AYER**
`Cavil at Rest`

## The Heat Lamp

I have always wanted
to get back to the days
where you're home is to never be alone
live with a generator feeling the buzz
from the shocks you absorb when you're getting a hug
and you can light up when you wake
before the showers that you take
or warm up while you stay up late
to prepare for the coming day
where you don't always get what you need
and the will to keep up is the will to succeed
and the measure of a man is weighted in the one he loves

now I live a different way
free from all her electricity
I run off a self-sufficient battery
that I keep from the promise of the way it would be
if she came back to find the answer was me
so I wait for her call
thinking of all our faults
and I finally let the light die out
to fess up

that what you want ain't always what we need
and maybe the collapse was in order to succeed
and the measure of a woman is hidden in the way she loves

by not loving anymore

## DAN LYMAN
### Halos

Loud bang on the window. 8 or 9 Hispanic men. Landscapers
again? This is getting old

So hot. Good day to go to Jones alone . . . Everyone else has a
real life. Sun.

Evening news called us "The BB Gun Bandits" The Fuzz called
us "lucky bastards"

Free The Kid

arm chair | couch | front seat | floor | Pacific Coast Highway |
bed's a luxury

12,000 feet. Unsuitable transportation. Exhilarating

" . . . you don't know where you're going, but you know where
you want to be."

Rug got pulled out. Coma months. Mad Dog 20/20 and fell to
pieces

Taken in by strangers . . . embraced changed endless gratitude

Came together

Not landing anytime soon: "Dear Lord, bring the angels
onboard."

Penetrating eyes and I've got to know more. You will, too

Can't forget your friends . . . even if they forget you.

Thank you, Rowland.

**KERRY TRUSEWICZ**
Royden

*Sometimes I Travel to You*

I
downing out for the evening to
desert fox, kind and fast jackrabbit,
leveled bird and fortress

then sleeping
then waking and yawning to calm swells
of our maiden pacific, fond gurgle and salty swing

"i'm easy" yes you are
as it's easy to be all in the airs
surrounding

II
my odd
conversation is delivered
to you via chirp

and the wired space
sets our untangled
fingers humming back
again

III
the stars at night
are big and bright
deep in the heart
of Utah

and the wood!

IV
do you ever feel like a good one?
i once bent petals in half and
stepped over flailing sparrow.

"i don't know. do i?"

**CHRISTOPHER JAMES RUFF**
**Kaddisfly**

## *Waves*

Apostolic
Beliefs
Conjure
Divine
Earthly
Faith,
Gainsaying
Heavenly
Intuition,
Juxtaposing
Kindred
Love.
Make
New
Opposition,
Providing
Quizzical
Rationality,
Stunning
Treasure,
Undying
Virtuous

Will,
XYZ . . .

No prophet has ever been accepted in his own village.

An owl on a hill knows the moon
and clear as a river,
like flowers we bloom faster when we're farther from the shade.

Before you grow old don't get snipped and sold.

So what about animals and all the poor starving souls? Is it
really worth our time?

Well, here's the thing with time . . .

It's our apartment, and rent is still due even when our skin skips
town.

Since we all are dealt zero sum hands we should have a little
compassion,
but people sure can be incompetent at understanding this
concept.

Be offended by the things we've done.
Be offended by the shade of our thumbs.
Be offended by just where we stand.

One day I swear . . .
No empire has ever been true to those that helped it begin.

## The Calm of Calamity

In the eye of the sky the night bent down and sighed,
and said with a smile, to the wind as it cried:

"Your tears form the oceans and as with the tides,
time forms the tears that you cast from your eyes,

your salt forms the land and the earth becomes mortar,
which dictates your path with direction and order,

as rivers lay softly asleep in their beds,
you cry with great plumage from violet to red,

as you to your sons and as you to your daughters,
I'll keep gentle watch over earth and its waters,

and as much as you control the ebb and the flow,
as sure as the currents carve pathways below,
as swift as the tides rotate from high to low,
that's as swift as you came and as quickly you'll go."

## Osmosis

.i wrote the dry spell

i built the fences
built the walls
chopped the wood
and poured concrete

i made the fortress around my hand
with frozen ink that melts to rain
which waters the root of thoughts and swells

as vines of words begin to overtake
my walls
my fence
my fortress
my hand
and with my watered pen

.i wrote the dry spell

.i wrote the dry spell

.i wrote the dry spell

## Alone as a Tree?

I gave a tree sight so it could see the earth its limbs and all its
leaves
The ground was there before its sight as were its roots before its
life
The tree gazed at the other trees with separate branches limbs
and leaves
And noticed different shades and widths that gave each unique
tree its niche

As the tree used its new pair of eyes it noticed unique shades
and lives
A thousand trunks born from the earth each tree alone in death
and birth
Blessed with sight the tree felt cursed and prayed to have its
gift reversed
Because it thought when one tree falls that other trees don't
care at all

From this point the tree proclaimed that selfish trees should be
ashamed
Because they stand alone and still as brothers fall and sisters wilt
They stand alone in sight and sound and never help the trees
around

They live to watch each other fall and never seem to care
at all

Before the tree gave up all hope and lost its will to thrive and
cope
I gave it sight right the ground and it saw roots connecting down
The same roots that were there since birth into the ground
unto the earth
The roots that stay vanished from sight but with the earth gave
the tree life

The tree then saw its roots are one with fellow trees though
separate trunks
And then it knew though separate leaves its roots belonged to
fellow trees
And it then knew when one tree falls that every tree holds a
slight pause
Because trees are one in death and birth connected by their
roots and earth

The tree learned that along with sight comes the pledge to use
it right
And not to judge based on what's seen because trees are not
such selfish beings
Although sight would have them stand alone when eyes are
closed each tree is home
Each tree alive unto the earth sharing its roots in death and
birth

Humans are trees with different leaves
With differing shades of which each one perceives
And as sight has them think they're alone in the breeze
Their roots form the words of soft prayers on their knees

**DANIEL MURILLO**
`Lorene Drive`

## *For the Rest of Us*

It seems like everybody knows
You're running in circles again
I fell into your perfect smile
No one should know about this
You keep your smile
I'll keep this to myself
You're a wonderful thing
And that's obvious but
Don't light that cigarette again
You don't need a second opinion
About anything or anyone at all
Seems like everybody knows
That you're not going to be around
This time next year
Front line demanding activity
The cash flow slows
And now they need your dream
You're giving me a heart attack
But we'll keep this to ourselves
So what was learned from this lesson
As I walked right through the room to you

**COLIN FRANGICETTO**
`Circa` `Survive`

## *"HUMILIATING SOBRIETY" and the MISSING LIMB (a godless prayer)*

PART I: Lying Asleep.

Woke up to feel something
missing like a limb.
Numb and black, the ever-growing void.
Like cancerous vines that strangle
the throat of memory.

Misplacement of the metaphysical microscope.
Overlooking closeness and
purpose like danger
and its apparent absence;
our hilarious helmet.

Dreamless and dry,
Sleepwalker countryside.
Suicide culture.
Bottle to the mouth.
Parasite to its host.
Pour into our bellies,
empty us out.

Plastic newspaper television warship
of the hijacked "reality."
Commanders in chief,
so-called "leaders of men."
The blackest of magic.
The blackest of hearts.

Gray-eyed demon tricksters.
Circus showmen selling flaccid insurance.
Insurance of madness. Insurance of fear. (keep angry and afraid)
Selling the mirage of a vanishing god.
Brought to our knees.
Abandoned we feel
everything in order
now faith is placed into them. (removed from our shoulders)

Enter through exit.
New objects of worship.
Meaningless logos,
the name-brand mentality,
toilet-water ministry.
Cut and paste, clone-like communities.
Terror alert watch, pepper-spray stock market.
Scared of the inevitable crash and ourselves.
Speeches of freedom in united division.
Social insecurity.
FeNcE after FeNcE after FeNcE after FeNcE.
Invisible families, impossible values.

Darkening spiral,
crystalline
cellophane, our **religion**.
Descending detachment,
most brutal of **drugs**.
Consumption of distraction; from ourselves,
from our **language**, and from communication itself.
It seems that words never reach   quite   f a r   enough.


PART II: Alarm.


Importance: the perverse arrangement.
Buried potential in deep, unmarked graves.
Forsaken, our families. Forsaken, our love.
Wearing ourselves like masks in the ritual.
Custom closing our circles, seemingly sealing our **fate**,
concealing the next notes of the octave.


Time: the unraveling string.
The knot twist eternal.
Intestines with wings.
Infinite loss. Infinite gain.
We wait for this **war** to be finally over.
We wait to be together again.
We wait for the **rebirth**.
We can no longer be waiting in vain.


Whispering to wizards,
Screaming to scribes.
Asking of artists,

the modern day shaman. (the most needed, the medicine man)
"Bring us back to life."
"Paint us back to life."
We long for completion,
begging the infinite questions.


Their answers are elegant.
Naked but secure,
The truth as it disrobes.
Hideous beauty. Complex simplicity.
These solutions sleep with our struggles, internal.
They breathe with and speak through
The mud, grass and trees, the swamps and the seas.
The sands of the lands and the stars never seen.


PART III: Lying Awake.


And they say . . .


"Remember your families.
Remember your love.
Tribute the ones who were here before,
you will join them like mold.
Teach to the young who will soon be the old.
Call out the cowards who claim falsely to lead.
Return to origin.
Return to intuition.
The sacred reunion.
Humanity and its soul,
the function of the wave.

Perception of the particle.

Beyond the subatomic quantum mechanical.

Passing through **flesh**. Into the **blood**. Under the **cells**.

This once was a 'flat world'

There is more to discover.

Although we fly, it ends in land or crash.

The freedom of flight means eventual choice.

Fall to the earth.

Look to the skies.

(Those streets that hold our spirits inside,

like lips that kiss for the first and the ultimate time.)

Our standards, our structures, (both physical and non)

must be torn down, seeding the future, cement to the past.

Lest it be forgotten, forever remember to always rebuild.

This time, build to last.

(What seems redundant is most likely just urgent.)

Resist what is known,

It betrays what is learned.

Resist what is owned,

It betrays what is needed."

Something is missing.

It seems after all,

that in fact we are all part of both

the limb that assumes disembodiment

and its forgetful owner gone numb.


This would have to mean . . .

**we are all somehow missing each other.**

**ANTHONY GREEN**
Circa Survive

## *Look—Look*

That's a shitty thing to say man, you're a shitty dude, you know
that? Nobody's special—and nobody changes. It's rare when we
can even tell the difference. I can't say I'm always happy with
who I am. But daily I'm at battle with a personal sense of defeat
I feel everyone's born with. Original sin. We are a result of
shame in motion, wet friction, fear, an impulse control board
located low, and underneath the belly. Processed—(pray for
forgiveness) and nurtured from what would seem by any child
to be a giant tittie, or denied the tittie. I'm not sure which is
worse. But I am sure that defeats the whole idea of special from
the get-go---------------------------------------------------Unless
you're retarded. Canal. Every sound amplified. Coming through.
The pulls and pushes. The air and bushes. Warm feet rub
against my feet. Small and walking with me passed our fifth
year. Look look—see that sleep drug commercial. Where all the
fluffy puppies rest curled up in the doggy bed. That look—look!
Like they're dead.

## BRENDAN EKSTROM
`Circa Survive`

*" . . . "*

The ringing in our ears was almost incidental. But the smell, as it slipped through the bathroom door, was too much to take. We stood there, crippled by silence, the smoke and sulfur stinging our eyes. And though it would take the shockwaves ten years to bring the arthritis to my knees, yours turned to stone that day, crumbling onto the tile. If only your son had been enough to keep you standing.

## ERIC FREDERIC
Facing New York

hands are lightbulbs
shattering from where they dock
every instant illuminated
on trains cutting through fields of boyish hair
inviting world leaders to walk on the glass
fingers are shards sprinkled in the shallow mud
refracting light with precision
so we can work after hours
this morning
i woke by the river
troubled, uneasy
i reach for my sneakers
totally soaked
and a boys' choir starts to sing
in a language i don't speak
because it's deer language
hundreds of faun
high in the branches
of the redwood trees
no expression, unmoving
just staring down at me
i've had a rough transition back into the states
japan was a bird i wanted to eat
but could never catch
let alone digest

once i'd seen another _____ of the world
i cried for my parents
in their modest home
just how my eyes grew eager to spill
at the movies
during the previews for that summer's blockbuster
i don't want to think about this anymore

## MATTHEW KELLY
The Autumns

### *The Pale Antechamber*

I once read a book entitled *House of Leaves*. It was, not surprisingly, about a house, though not an ordinary one. This house's interior measured larger than its exterior. On learning this, the owner was naturally spooked. This rather enticing opener was shortly derailed and the plot soon ramified to a delta of dead ends and failed twists. The anchoring of the uncanny in things as banal as a house and tape measure, however, was a stroke of genius.

Lately, I have started to wonder if the author might have been writing from experience. I will explain why in a moment. But first, some background is in order. We begin with what I assume is a rarely expressed but widely appreciated truth. People enjoy listening to other people having sex. It sounds nice. It pulses like *Urstoff* on a clear blue morning. It is warm and inviting. This is not to say that everyone is an *active* voyeur, only that everyone is a voyeur. I, for one, am always pleased to have neighbors who screw loudly and often. I especially relish listening to the girl.

I noticed a few months ago that I have once again been lucky enough to have such neighbors. They get going late at night, usually between two and three in the morning, suffusing the walls of the apartment building with such a fever that they seem to sweat. I am certain their young moans raise the temperature of all in earshot.

One morning, I mentioned to my wife, "You know, our neighbors fuck like mad. Just about every night at the same time."

"You enjoy that, don't you?" she replied insinuatingly.

"Of course," I said.

"Do you know which neighbors?" she asked.

"On the other side of the bedroom." I pointed. "You can hear everything. These walls are like paper."

"You're confused," she stated nonchalantly. "An old man lives next door—very old. And he lives alone."

She then reminded me of a recent occurrence that, on reflection, threw my theory into disarray. A vagrant had wandered behind our apartment complex early one Saturday and began banging on doors and rattling windows, looking for a handout. Our aged neighbor made his way to the back door noisily and scolded him. "I'm an old man. I don't have anything for you. Leave me alone!"

"Give me a hat!" the vagrant demanded.

"I don't *have* a hat!" barked our hapless neighbor. "Why do I need a hat? I don't go outside."

This did seem to discredit my claim. It was hardly plausible that this fellow enjoyed a thriving and utterly punctual sex life. On consideration, I figured that the sounds were probably coming from upstairs, or maybe from the apartment that stood catty-corner to ours. But after a few days' reprieve, the stirring and moaning began anew and, to my surprise, the action was definitely happening in the room opposite ours. Doubly intrigued, I raised myself on one elbow, placing one ear to the wall and plugging the other to fully exploit my auditory powers. I suddenly heard nothing. Reclining again, I could just make out a news program blasting from a cheap, tinny radio. And there beneath the coarsened hum of today's events were the unmistakable sounds of you-know-what. This time, however, there was a distinctly pornographic tinge to the proceedings. The bad music was an immediate giveaway. Add to that the boilerplate naughty chatter and it became clear that the old man was, for whatever reason, orchestrating a Janus-faced news-porn symphony. Maybe he had a crush on one of the anchors. "They are getting sexier," I thought. On the other hand, he was easily eighty-five. I now faced the gruesome specter of an old, old porn aficionado. The mystery was solved, at any rate. No young couples were tangling on the floor of this ailing character's apartment.

Or so I thought. Months later, it started again. This time, the porn hypothesis was jettisoned straightaway. No music. No dirty talk. Just those familiar and eminently alluring sounds of pleasure. It was, to repeat, all transpiring on the other side of the bedroom wall. Lounging in my bed, imbibing these sweet sounds, I realized something: my head was attached to the wall. Curious, I removed it. This yielded silence. I reattached, and the sex returned. I repeated the exercise several times more, perplexed by my ability to toggle so cleanly between the two. From my limited knowledge of acoustics, I could gather that such proximate sounds should at least have been detectable without my having to place my head against the bedroom wall. I could not account for it, and trying to fatigued me. I soon fell asleep.

I had almost forgotten this bizarre nocturnal quandary when

I ran into our landlord one afternoon a few days later. Half the power in our apartment had mysteriously flickered out. The landlord and his affable engineer friend came by to investigate. Unable to help myself, I asked at what seemed an opportune moment, "Who lives next door to us?"

"You mean there?" he said, nodding hastily in the relevant direction.

"Yes," I answered.

He stared at me quizzically for a moment and then replied, "No one lives there. It's been vacant for over a year."

Dumbstruck and a little breathless, I heard myself ask, "Who is the old man?"

The landlord shot me a bemused and vaguely condescending look, then rejoined the electrician without offering a reply.

I was, needless to say, unsatisfied and now deeply perplexed. I challenged my wife. "You see, something weird *is* going on. We saw an old man come out of that apartment!"

"We didn't *see* him, we *heard* him. He's probably from one of the other apartments and it just sounded like he was next door," she reassured me.

I didn't push the point, but I knew something was amiss. I tried not to let curiosity get the better of me but it was no use. In short order, I found myself outside the next-door window, peaking through the blinds to catch sight of the old man. Our apartment building sits on the corner of Orange and Franklin in Hollywood, in the shade of the Magic Castle. One can look into the apartments either from the Orange side, which opens to an all but fixed concatenation of cars and the occasional red double-decker that line the street.

Alternatively, one can view the apartments from Franklin. From this side, many of them are tucked out of sight, their back windows winding behind the building. For several weeks that summer, I could be glimpsed out front in the early morning hours, pretending to water my phantom neighbor's flowers while furtively peering through the front windows. I kept such espionage beneath the umbrella of night, of course, but partook so routinely in this mischief that I remained eminently vulnerable to detection (and perhaps eviction, having already made a fine impression on the landlord with my impossible line of inquiry).

In retrospect, though, I can hardly fault myself. I would lie down in bed, begin drifting off, and then, like clockwork, the noises would rouse me. I would press my ear to the wall to no avail. I would relax again, letting my head touch the wall, and there it would be. Some nights I would only hear the blaring of news programs or sitcoms. Others it would be the sex. Still others the pornography. Bewildered, I would invariably sneak outside and peer into the old man's apartment, only to stare vainly into a hopelessly darkened room.

And so I was forced to reckon with a rather inscrutable set of facts. One: the adjacent apartment was vacant. Two: an insomniac, porn-addicted old man resided there, occasionally playing host to live sex. Three: this was detectable only when lying face up on the bed and touching the crown of one's head to the bedroom wall.

Later, a fourth pear-shaped premise would be thrown into the mix: the head had to be mine. When my wife tried it, she heard nothing.

The palpable presence of unreality did not persist long without consequence. I was soon unhorsed and scrambling for inconceivably scattered first principles. Such was my state when the still more unsettling solution dawned on me like the rising sun of genius. I had, I realized, stumbled upon a portal to my own mind. Indeed, the portal was located exactly four feet and three inches across and two feet and seven and a quarter inches up my wall. I marked it with a pencil. It was also time-sensitive. Touching the top of my skull to the penciled dot between two and three in the morning would unfailingly do the trick. The room next door would briefly double as the chamber of my subconscious. Not being a psychologist by training, I could not unearth the deeper meaning of its occupants: a three-legged octogenarian, pacing the pale antechamber of death; a young couple, entwined in the sunlit ecstasy of sex; and the fuzzy ambience of porn, news, and indecipherable chatter in which both bathed.

## DAVID MELILLO

I went down to the bar but they would'nt let me near
They said "Son your'e much too young to be hanging around
here"
So, I went down to the park but they soon turned me away
They said "Surely you've got better things to do with all your
days"
You see I've tried to find a place between the boys and men
Many have tried and few have survived or been heard from
again
I had no such luck,
So I just light one up,
As I watch life pass me by.

It always burns, no matt what.

Your esophagus feels like its on fire, and you can't help but wince and pound your fist on the table.

Why do we put ourselves through it then?

I'm not entirely sure but I'm guessing it has something to do with rights of passage and all of that high school bullshit that I say I don't believe in . . .

I don't do it much, if at all anymore, because there isn't anyone around to impress and I know that if I'm drinking its only to forget about things that should be dealt with in a fashionable manner. .

.Never mind that last comment; its way too pretentious and I'm really trying to avoid that kind of thing.

What I'm trying to get at . . . what am I trying to get at?

I'm actually trying to fill out the hours of a car ride into Connecticut with some nostalgia that was conjured up by the weather this time of year in upstate New York.

Back in Florida we don't have seasons, only palm trees and humidity.

This apathy just doesn't help at all
And now this barricade has turned into a wall
But, honestly, what can I do?
It makes it much harder when they're laughing at you
Everyone around me seems aware
Of a secret that they do not care to share
But oh, I dare not speak out
For if they know that I am weak I'm down and out

So I'm making a name
I'm staking in a claim in what I knew was mine all along
I'll fake it for fame
I do not know shame and I would sell my soul for a song

**TIM McILRATH**
Rise Against

## *babygirl*

i don't know your laugh
i don't know your cry
and sometimes your face is a memory
through my fingers you slip
again, but like the first time
it stings like a needle sewing right through me
but we were in love!
i remember it well
and they can't ever take that from me
day after day and night after night
i wake up; my arms still empty

oh babygirl, has it really been this long?
oh babygirl, i'm coming home.

a voice on the phone
a face in a frame
a postcard from thousands of miles away
a breath that I hold
in fear that one day
i'll be met with a blank stare on her face
but we were in love!

for a moment at least!
i swear to God she knew me
words I won't hear
and things I won't see
the steps you took; but not to me

oh babygirl, has it really been this long?
oh babygirl, i'm coming home
oh babygirl, when did your hair get so long?
oh babygirl, i'm coming home.

**MIKE MADRUGA**

## *Owl Farm*

To all who witness, tip your cocktails in honor
As the ashes bleed into the clouds
And bite your lip and tremor in horror
As the body parts rain down

Something great has died today
Left its marking on the wall
Every outlaw in line is in disarray
Their king has abandoned them all

The shot sent the owls afoot from their trees
And echoed the valley with a terrible blast
All who heard knew what had come to be
And feared their hero did not last

Can't you see the season is over
No point in existing
He screams fire with breath
Of whiskey, gun powder, and mescaline

Owl Farm seems much quieter now
And all ascend the cliffs to see
The empty valley where the fist rises with power
Cursing all who doubt with reprieve

**LUIS DUBUC**
The Secret Handshake

## *Last Day Alive*

What could I do?
Feeling free. Do I try to make my peace?
Do I spend the time with my family?
One more day to make love to you.
Did I leave my mark on the world?
Did I learn to fly? Did I live out my dreams?
Did I change anyone's life?
Am I happy?
I feel a sense of calm come over me.
It's just after sunset and I'm feeling sleepy.
I've climbed to the highest point in this damned city.
I never really liked it much, but I'm afraid I'm going to miss it.
Hold my hand as I look at the stars one last time.
My whole life I struggled to find my voice and now it's almost
gone.
It was a good game, we had fun. We tried our best,
it's my last day alive.

# ABOUT THE EDITOR

Rich Balling's foundation as a professional musician began with a five-year stint in the ska/indie rock group RX Bandits, whose influence has had an immeasurable effect on their respective realm of independent music. After releasing three albums with the band (and playing on countless other projects, including a multiplatinum album with The Bloodhound Gang) Balling sauntered into other aspects of the music industry, dabbling in a slew of progressive side projects and spearheading the collaboration of the much-anticipated progressive rock groups The Sound of Animals Fighting and Cowboy Communist. Balling acted as editor and contributor to the band poetry anthology *Revolution on Canvas,* Volume One. Balling's extensive knowledge of music, combined with his raucous and raw accounts of the road, the industry, and the subtle threads that bind the network of modern American music, lend to the bold and purposeful dynamism of his professional demeanor. He lives in Texas, and is also a bit of a hypochondriac.

# ARTIST CONTACT INFO

KELCEY AYER
www.cavilatrest.com

RICH BALLING
www.thesoundofanimalsfighting.com

AARON BARRETT
www.reelbigfish.com

AARON BEDARD
www.banecentral.com

SAL BOSSIO
www.envyonthecoast.com

M. S. BREEN
www.thisisemanuel.com

BRENDAN BROWN
www.thereceivingendofsirens.com

JOE BROWN
www.astaticlullaby.com

TRAVIS BRYANT
www.goodbyetomorrow.com

AARON CHAPMAN
www.nursesmusic.com

CHI CHENG
www.deftones.com

STEVE CHOI
www.rxbandits.com

SCHUYLAR CROOM
www.heislegend.com

BOBBY DARLING
www.gatsbysamericandream.com

DAMON DAW
www.nursesmusic.com

JARED DRAUGHON
www.classiccase.net

LUIS DUBUC
www.thesecrethandshake.net

BRENDAN EKSTROM
www.circasurvive.com

STEVE ELKINS
www.theautumns.com

MATT EMBREE
www.rxbandits.com

DIA FRAMPTON
www.meganddia.com

MEG FRAMPTON
www.meganddia.com

CHRIS FRANGICETTO
www.daysawaymusic.com

COLIN FRANGICETTO
www.circasurvive.com

ERIC FREDERIC
www.facingnewyork.com

JASON GLEASON
www.actionreactionmusic.com

ANTHONY GREEN
www.circasurvive.com

SHAWN HARRIS
www.thematches.com

ALEX HOVIS
www.papermodelsmusic.com

KIRK HUFFMAN
www.gatsbysamericandream.com

RYAN HUNTER
www.envyonthecoast.com

ELGIN JAMES
www.elginjames.com

EVAN JEWETT
myspace.com/workbeebuzz

JERRY JONES
www.trophyscars.com

REBEKAH JORDAN
www.rebekahjordanmusic.com

BEN JORGENSEN
www.armorforsleep.com

MATTHEW KELLY
www.theautumns.com

ALEXANDER KENT
www.sayanythingmusic.com

JESSE KURVINK
www.hellogoodbye.net

STEVEN LEFEBVRE
www.sophiarock.com

DAN LYMAN
myspace.com/halosband

MIKE MADRUGA
www.marchofflames.com

NICK MARTIN
www.underminded.com

JONAH MATRANGA
www.jonahmatranga.com

TIM McILRATH
www.riseagainst.com

PORTER McKNIGHT
www.atreyurock.com

DAVID MELILLO
www.davemelillo.com

ROBERT MORRIS
www.thehushsound.com

DANIEL MURILLO
www.lorenedrive.com

BOB NANNA
www.bobnanna.com

JOHN NOLAN
www.straylightrun.com

DUANE OKEN
   www.socraticmusic.com

CRAIG OWENS
   www.chiodos.net

RICH PALMER
   www.purevolume.com/buddah

ADAM PANIC
   www.adampanic.com

JOSH PARTINGTON
   www.firescapeband.com

JUSTIN PIERRE
   www.motioncitysoundtrack.com

BRANDON RIKE
   www.deadpoetic.com

MARK ROSE
   www.spitalfield.net

CHRISTOPHER JAMES RUFF
   www.kaddisfly.com

GRETA SALPETER
   www.thehushsound.com

GABE SAPPORTA
   www.cobrastarship.com

DANNY SMITH
   www.thecitydrivemusic.com

BRIAN TASCH
   myspace.com/boyarmageddonrulez

JARROD TAYLOR
   www.inreverentfear.com

NICK THOMAS
www.thespillcanvas.com

JOHN TRAN
myspace.com/j2themotherfuckingtran

RYAN TRASTER
myspace.com/smalltownsburnalittleslower

KERRY TRUSEWICZ
www.roydenstork.com

JON TUMMILLO
www.follynj.com

ADAM TURLA
www.murderbydeath.com

KENNY VASOLI
www.startinglinerock.com

ERIC VICTORINO
www.stratadirect.com

SCOTT WALDMAN
www.thecitydrivemusic.com

PETER WENTZ
website.falloutboyrock.com

BRANDON WRONSKI
myspace.com/eyealaska

# PERMISSIONS

"Annalisa" copyright © 2007 by Justin Pierre; "Speech to Text, Thought to Action" copyright © 2007 by Jonah Matranga; "I am right-handed." copyright © 2007 by Rebekah Jordan; "About Me:" copyright © 2007 by John Tran; "Of ritual and habit I opened my mouth" copyright © 2007 by Brendan Brown; "Letter to a Gypsy" copyright © 2007 by Schuylar Croom; "Lao-tzu and a Friend Play a Game of Marbles" and "Dalí" copyright © 2007 by Vincent Reyes; "For the first time, this sickness . . ." copyright © 2007 by Meg Frampton; "Hospitals Always Smell Like Decaying Hair" copyright © 2007 by Dia Frampton; "27 Hours" and "Orchids" copyright © 2007 by Josh Partington; "New York City Vampires" and "Human Error" copyright © 2007 by Jared Draughon; "The Study" copyright © 2007 by Colleen Napolitano; "Einstein on the Beach" "Werner Herzog" "Sarah Kane" "H. P. Lovecraft" "Calvino" and "Celine" copyright © 2007 by Rich Balling; "For the Day" "It May as Well Have Been March 21, 1982." and "If Humans Have Heartbeats, Do Robots Have Heartbeeps?" copyright © 2007 by Jason Gleason; "A Short Clip from 'The Unlikeliness of Counterpane'" copyright © 2007 by Alexander Kent; "A Young Mother's Medicine" copyright © 2007 by Jarrod Taylor; "The Big

Reveal" copyright © 2007 by Ben Jorgensen; "Do What You Need to Be Happy" copyright © 2007 by Rich Palmer; "Come tell me old man" copyright © 2007 by Porter McKnight; "My apartment was muggy when I awoke" copyright © 2007 by Kirk Huffman; "Never Forget Her" copyright © 2007 by Alex Hovis; "You are the moon" and "New Year's Eve" copyright © 2007 by Greta Salpeter; "the mess i've made for you" and "the sinking of some great ship" copyright © 2007 by Rob Morris; "Is Bette Midler a True Star?" copyright © 2007 by Scott Waldman; "Hesperia" copyright © 2007 by Danny Smith; "save the boy" and "missouri" copyright © 2007 by Travis Bryant; "I spoke with GOD last night . . ." copyright © 2007 by Aaron Chapman; "Musicalism" copyright © 2007 by Damon Daw; "My Flaws Get Along" copyright © 2007 by Kenny Vasoli; "I was eight years old when . . ." copyright © 2007 by Elgin James; "One Summer Knight" copyright © 2007 by Aaron Bedard; "Auditions with Our Heavenly Father" copyright © 2007 by Ryan Hunter; "My heart is pounding the whole way there." copyright © 2007 by Sal Bossio; "Tonight we lie in a city . . ." copyright © 2007 by Peter Wentz; "Dramatic Monologue" copyright © 2007 by China Soul; "Roll Up My Sympathy" copyright © 2007 by Matthew Roskowski; "Which Way?" copyright © 2007 by Matthew Clegg; "Vocals/Guitar" copyright © 2007 by Mark Rose; "feeding bob potter" copyright © 2007 by Steve Lefebvre; "The Death of a Family Guilt" and "Murder, Prostitution and Other Forms of Democracy and the Institution of Marriage" copyright © 2007 by Chi Cheng; "Progress in Part" "Sand in Context" and "Kodiak" copyright © 2007 by Brandon Wronski; "Hello me." copyright © 2007 by Adam Panic; "I Might Be Wrong" copyright © 2007 by John Nolan; "My Doe" and accompanying artwork copyright © 2007 by Shawn Harris; "Death Rattle" copyright © 2007 by Ryan